THE
bundt®
COLLECTION

131 RECIPES FOR THE
BUNDT CAKE BAKER

BRIAN HART HOFFMAN

THE
bundt®
COLLECTION

131 RECIPES FOR THE BUNDT CAKE BAKER

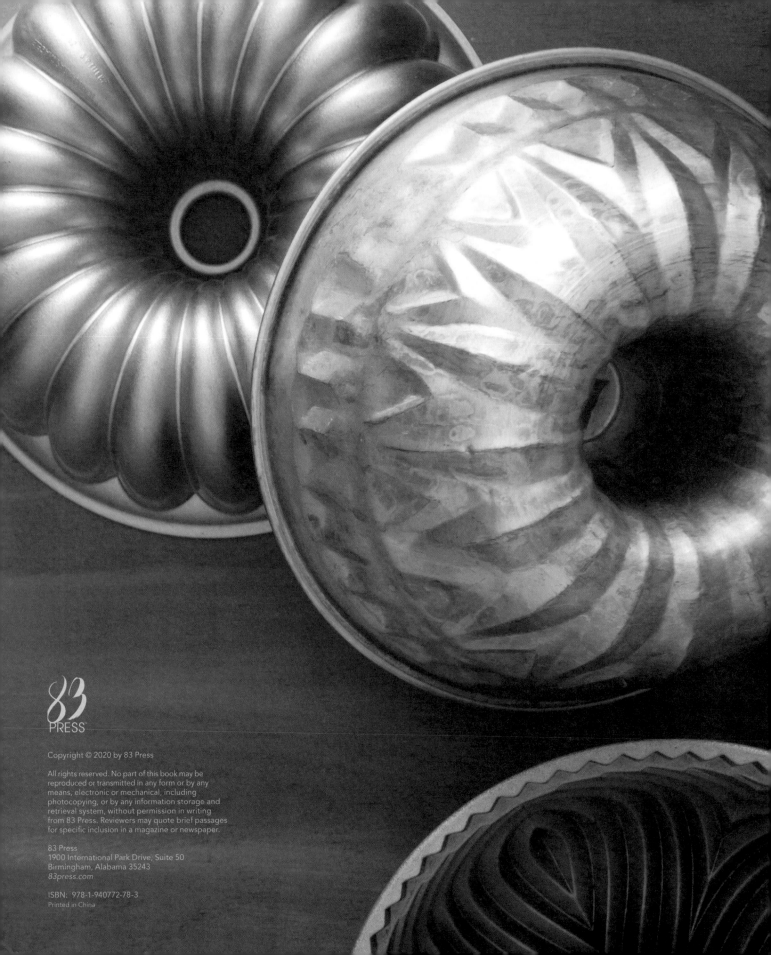

83 Press
1900 International Park Drive, Suite 50
Birmingham, Alabama 35243
83press.com

ISBN: 978-1-940772-78-3
Printed in China

contents

8 PREFACE

10 FOREWORD

14 THE PAN THAT STARTED A BAKING REVOLUTION
Discover the story behind Nordic Ware and the iconic pan on which this cookbook is based

24 PAN POWER
Check out the epic Bundt pans used in this cookbook

26 ESSENTIAL BUNDT TOOLS
This is the equipment you need for baking beautiful Bundt cakes every time

28 CHOCOLATE INDULGENCE
From a Rocky Road Bundt Cake to a German Chocolate Cake with Butterscotch Glaze, chocolate takes center stage in these recipes

52 SPIKED WITH SPIRITS
Boozy Bundt cakes galore! If you like your cake with a kick, this is the chapter for you.

78 FABULOUS & FRUITY
Filled with fresh fruit and jammy centers, these fruit-forward Bundts are sure to bring brightness to your kitchen

104 SWIRLED & TWIRLED
The most showstopping Bundt cakes of them all—these recipes feature beautiful marbled designs and surprise-center fillings, from a Peanut Butter and Jelly Bundt Cake to a strawberry swirl masterpiece

122 POUND CAKE PERFECTION
We pay tribute to one of the most classic cakes

148 SPICE IS NICE
These Bundt cakes brim with all the most aromatic, soul-warming spices

170 A YEAR OF BUNDTS
Here, discover a Bundt cake recipe for every month of the year

199 RECIPE INDEX

BAKE FROM SCRATCH IS BIG ON BUNDTS.

Bundt cakes are timeless. You can find a recipe for one in almost every issue of *Bake from Scratch*, and we've even had a Bundt cake cover star a few times. For me, the Bundt cake is my go-to one-layer stunner, steeped in fond memories and an opportunity to highlight my favorite flavors. Why? Simply put, the Bundt is an icon, a beacon to bakers everywhere. Since its release in 1950, Nordic Ware's Bundt pan has inspired thousands of bakers to embrace the simple elegance of a one-layer cake with a gorgeous design baked right in. As a versatile blank canvas, the original Bundt pan has led to the most whimsical of creations, like the Tunnel of Fudge Cake. Yet with each new design Nordic Ware releases, from the sharply ridged Bavaria Bundt Pan to the delicately curved Swirl Bundt Pan, more delicious innovation follows.

An ode to the Bundt cake, this cookbook is brimming with exciting all-new recipes guaranteed to up your Bundt baking game, along with all-time favorites that you'll turn to time and time again. Beyond amazing recipes, we arm you with insightful tips and tricks from our test kitchen and share the game-changing baking equipment you need to bake perfect Bundt cakes every time.

Each chapter of this cookbook shows what magic a Bundt pan can bring to the table. In our "Chocolate Indulgence" chapter, we have black cocoa, white chocolate, and chopped chocolate working in concert with classics like carrot cake, coconut, and chai spice. In our "Fabulous & Fruity" collection, sweet summer stone fruit, fall harvest-fresh apples, and zesty winter citrus pump up the seasonal flavor of each cake. I grew up in the South, where Bundt cakes have always been the crowning achievement of a holiday dinner or brunch spread. Our "Pound Cake Perfection" chapter is an ode to some of the most nostalgic incarnations of Bundt cakes, from rich cream cheese pound cakes to a tropical coconut take. As the Bundt pan offers the perfect mold for decadent, dense cakes destined for thick glazes and syrup soaks, our "Spiked with Spirits" chapter packs the boozy punch you'll be craving for an adult treat. "Spice is Nice" is the chapter for those looking for that seductive hit of sweet heat. From a rum cake twist on banana bread to a sliceable revamp of the Dark 'n Stormy cocktail, this chapter is my favorite way to enjoy happy hour. In "Swirled & Twirled," all of the Bundt cakes hide a two-toned surprise, with fillings and batters swirled inside in a mesmerizing fashion. And in "A Year of Bundts," we offer a Bundt cake for every month, from a celebratory mimosa-infused beauty to a cream cheese-swirled red velvet cake.

Bakers are constantly inspired by ingredients, but in this cookbook, our recipes are as much inspired by the pan as they are the fruit, spices, and mix-ins we use. We created a cherries jubilee cake to go into Nordic Ware's lovely Jubilee Bundt Pan, and we gave the Elegant Party Bundt Pan the rainbow sprinkle-packed delight it deserves. I was particularly inspired by the Brilliance Bundt Pan, with its jet engine-like shape, to create the In-Flight Bundt Cake, a coffee and spiced cookie homage to my past career as a flight attendant.

It's funny to think how one iconic pan could inspire thousands of incredible recipes. But when bakers look at an empty Bundt pan sitting on the counter, we all think the same thing: sweet possibility.

FOREWORD

Sometimes, the simplest pleasures in life can also be the most satisfying. While we all know the feeling of immense gratification after baking (and serving to friends!) an exquisitely complex dessert prepared with multiple steps and hours of painstaking effort, we wouldn't be acknowledging reality if we didn't also admit to those moments when, just a half hour before our guests arrived for dinner, we wished we had chosen a simpler recipe, one we were confident would yield picture-perfect results.

Enter the Bundt cake. With its smooth, evenly browned crust; moist, dense crumb; and beautifully simple shape, it's no wonder this dessert with a hole in the middle has become the quintessential American cake for gatherings of all varieties, no matter the season. They're simple to bake, require relatively easy-to-source ingredients, are rarely dry or crumbly, and—perhaps best of all—need little to no decoration. Just a dusting of confectioners' sugar, a drizzle of vanilla glaze, or a ribbon of ganache, and you're ready for showtime.

My grandparents, Dave and Dotty Dalquist, founded Nordic Ware in 1946 in the basement of their home in Minneapolis, Minnesota. The Bundt came along in the early 1950s at the request of some local women from the Hadassah society who longed for a lighter-weight version of their heavy cast-iron gugelhupf pans from Europe. My grandfather delivered on their request with a cast-aluminum pan; however, because very few recipes existed for this type of pan, the Bundt did not initially see success. It wasn't until 1966 when the now-famous Tunnel of Fudge Cake won second prize in the Pillsbury Bake-Off competition that the Bundt was firmly cemented into baking culture across the nation. As testament to this, several

"A BUNDT CAKE HAS THE BEAUTY BAKED RIGHT INTO IT, THANKS TO THE INTRICATE DETAILS OF THE PAN ITSELF."

---

of our original cast Bundts have a permanent place in the Smithsonian Museum of American History in an exhibit that highlights how our country's eating habits and food preparation techniques have evolved over the past century.

My grandfather had a favorite saying about Bundts: "You don't have to be a fancy baker to bake a fancy cake." A Bundt cake has the beauty baked right into it, thanks to the intricate details of the pan itself. It's a cake meant to be shared and enjoyed with a group of people, whether that be family, friends, neighbors, or complete strangers. Simply put, Bundt cakes exude warmth and bring people together.

My grandmother, who was as much an integral part of building the Bundt legacy as my grandfather, toiled away in the kitchen on top of raising four children, creating literally hundreds of Bundt recipes over her lifetime to be used in conjunction with our famous pans. Though tastes have evolved with time and baking trends have shifted, many of Dotty's recipes remain the inspiration for today's modern Bundt recipes, and that legacy will likely live on for generations as young bakers try to recreate favorite recipes they remember from their parents and grandparents. If my grandfather were still alive, I know he would be so pleased to know that Bundt cakes continue to be enjoyed by millions of people around the world each and every day.

As the saying goes, "Simplicity is the ultimate form of sophistication," and what better dessert to exemplify this phrase than a Bundt cake, lovingly baked from scratch in your home kitchen.

—Jennifer Dalquist
Nordic Ware Executive Vice President of Sales and Marketing and Third-Generation Leader

THE PAN THAT STARTED A
BAKING REVOLUTION

WITH ONE ICONIC CAKE PAN, A MINNESOTA MAN CEMENTED HIS PLACE IN THE AMERICAN
BAKING TRADITION AND ESTABLISHED A POWERHOUSE THAT REMAINS FAMILY-OWNED
AND THE GO-TO BRAND FOR HOME BAKERS AROUND THE WORLD

PHOTOGRAPHY BY ELIESA JOHNSON

It's simple, ring-shaped, and all-American, with sculpted curves and a perfectly golden crust—no frills or frosting required. The Bundt is elegant yet effortless. For more than half a century, it's been a staple at potluck picnics, holiday meals, and every celebration in between.

The 1960s saw many changes, and for bakers, one of those was the breakthrough of the Bundt. It proved that one doesn't have to be a skilled baker to bake a beautiful cake. At the peak of Bundt mania, Nordic Ware, the pan's purveyor, was cranking out 30,000 pans a week and still couldn't make enough to keep department store shelves stocked. Today, the Bundt pan is the top-selling cake pan in the world. Two out of three kitchens in America have one, and you can even go see Nordic Ware's original prototype at the Smithsonian's National Museum of American History.

Our beloved Bundt pan's origin can be traced back to 1950, when several members of the Minneapolis, Minnesota, Haddassah, a Jewish women's group, approached then-fledgling business owner H. David Dalquist. The women wanted Dave to create a lighter, easier-to-handle version of the traditional ring-shaped pan used to bake a dense Central European cake known as gugelhupf or *kugelhupf*. The women referred to the cake as *Bund*, the German term for "gathering," as a nod to how the dessert was served to groups of people. The Old-World "Bund" pans were either overly fragile ceramic molds or heavy, clunky cast-iron.

It was only four years earlier, in 1946, that Dave and his wife, Dotty, the daughter of two Danish immigrants, started Nordic Ware in the basement of their Minneapolis home, manufacturing niche Scandinavian kitchenware items. Dave, whose parents were Swedish, was a chemical engineer with a specialty in metallurgy. The handful of cookware products he made were designed for Nordic delicacies like the *krumkake* (a crisp Norwegian cookie) iron and the *ebelskiver* (a Danish filled pancake) pan. In 1948, Dave built the official Nordic Ware headquarters in a suburb on the western side of Minneapolis called St. Louis Park, an area with a tightly knit Jewish community. Nordic Ware still operates out of St. Louis Park today.

As they sat in Dave's office, the women listed what the pan would need in order to successfully bake their beloved cake. It had to be round and deep, they said, with a tube running up the center of the mold to prevent an underbaked cake and support the large amount of batter needed to feed a crowd. Dave never shied away from a challenge.

Dotty posing with Nordic Ware products for an advertisement in 1960.

The pan that changed American baking. Nordic Ware currently offers 110 different shapes of cast-aluminum Bundt pans.

He designed a shorter, rounder version of the kugelhopf pan and revamped the original look, giving the pan more fluting, with alternating large and small scallops. Because it was lightweight yet sturdy and conducted heat evenly, Dave cast the pan in aluminum. As a final flourish, he added a "t" to the end of "Bund" to trademark it.

The best thing about Dave's pan was the cake it produced: a ready-made showpiece with well-defined curves and a graphic, captivating design baked right into the crust. Cutting into the cake's equally spaced lines made slicing portions a breeze. "Suddenly, there was a cake pan that baked the detail and design right into the cake, so anyone from a novice to an experienced baker could create something beautiful," says Jenny Dalquist, Dave and Dotty's granddaughter and Nordic Ware's executive vice president of sales and marketing.

Nonetheless, the pan looked different than anything the American bakeware market had seen. When the general manager at the plant first saw the prototype, he told Dave, "If you can sell that thing, you can sell anything." It was an inauspicious omen. Dave added the pan to the product line, but Nordic Ware barely made any profit from it for 16 years.

Flash forward to 1966. At the 17th annual Pillsbury Bake-Off Contest, Ella Helfrich of Houston, Texas, won second place for a Bundt cake called the Tunnel of Fudge. It had a gooey chocolate center that only a Bundt pan could render. The recipe—and the Bundt pan—went the 1960s version of viral. The cake and its pan appealed to a new generation of women who were going back to school and starting careers, with limited time spent in the kitchen. Overnight, Pillsbury received more than 200,000 letters from home bakers asking where they could get a Bundt pan. Bundt sales flourished for the next two decades. Nordic Ware has sold 70 million Bundts to date and inspired a host of imitators.

While they're known as "the Bundt people," Nordic Ware is so much more. Before the Bundt pan, 72 years ago in 1946, Dave returned home from World War II, having served as a radar technician for the United States Navy. With postwar spirits high, Dave knew he wanted to start his own business manufacturing a product that would be useful to society. With a family tree's worth of Danish recipes and a passion for baking, Dotty had the idea to create bakeware. With $500 in the bank, they began. Minneapolis was host to a vibrant community of immigrants from northern and central Europe, including Germans, Norwegians, Swedes, and the Dutch, and their descendants. But even with a built-in audience, things were tough during those early years.

They were often underfinanced, and Dave worked around the clock to make ends meet. Dotty, now 94, did her share, too. None of Dave's creations made it to the Nordic Ware product line before being tested by Dotty first. She was Nordic Ware's entire public relations and quality control program, and she knew each product just as well as the engineer who created it.

On the weekends, the Dalquist family traveled to trade shows and fairs to demonstrate the products. They'd load up in their station wagon and strap the show booth to the top of the car. "We waited years to get into the big Housewares Show in Chicago, Illinois, and there is a picture of Dave there the first year we attended that captures his spirit so well," Dotty says. "The booth was under a staircase, but you can see in his face how proud and hopeful he was for all that was to come."

The sudden success of the Bundt pan in the '60s allowed Nordic Ware to pursue new products, bigger retailers, and more markets, including microwave cookery. During the 1980s and 1990s, many of Nordic Ware's competitors moved manufacturing overseas for less-expensive labor. Conversely, Nordic Ware was and is committed to keeping their production in the United States. "It's not only about the 400 people we provide jobs for," Jenny says. "Our impact is even greater when you consider the domestic supply chain we source materials from. It's more far-reaching than you'd imagine."

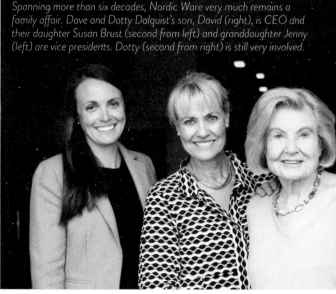

Spanning more than six decades, Nordic Ware very much remains a family affair. Dave and Dotty Dalquist's son, David (right), is CEO and their daughter Susan Brust (second from left) and granddaughter Jenny (left) are vice presidents. Dotty (second from right) is still very involved.

Nordic Ware is as devoted to keeping it in the family as they are to keeping the company in the States. Dotty is still involved and serves on Nordic Ware's board. Dave and Dotty's daughter Susan Brust is a vice president. Their two other daughters, Linda Jeffrey and Corrine Lynch, are on the board, and one grandchild leads Nordic Ware's process engineering team, helping automate production of key products. The company's family dynamic extends beyond the Dalquists. Many employees have been with Nordic Ware for 30 years or more, and some are second-generation. "I like to think that we have a culture where everyone within the factory considers their coworkers their family, too," says David Dalquist, Dave and Dotty's son, who has served as Nordic Ware's CEO since 1981. There's a sense of nurturing at Nordic Ware. Employees have flexible work hours, a summertime employee garden to grow and harvest vegetables and flowers, and an optional weekly Bundt Boot Camp workout class with a personal trainer.

The Dalquists' dedication to quality has never wavered either. Nordic Ware continually sets the bakeware bar in design, functionality, and ease of use. As some bakeware companies keep thinning products down to make them lighter, Nordic Ware has retained the heavier cast-aluminum material because it's durable and withstands years of use. Since steel is less expensive, many kitchenware manufacturers use it to make their products. But steel doesn't bake as well or render the crisp detail that cast aluminum does. Nordic Ware is also the only manufacturer making their pans out of cast aluminum with nonstick coating, so the pans will pop out perfect cake shapes without sticking.

Every 2.3 seconds, somewhere in the world, someone buys a Nordic Ware product. With products sold in more than 30 countries, the wide range of kitchenware items (almost 400) includes everything from grilling accessories to woks. But of all of Nordic Ware's products, none has made a larger cultural impact than the Bundt pan.

"When I was a teenager, my dad would take me on sales calls, and I'd listen to him talking to the customer so passionately about all the attributes of this pan and I'd start blushing," David says. "I'd say, 'Dad, it's just a pan. It can't be that special.' I couldn't have been more wrong."

Though Dave never baked a cake in his life, Dotty says, he filled a domestic void bakers never even knew existed. He believed in the power of gathering family and friends around dessert. And that's something we can get behind.

A BUNDT PAN COMES TO LIFE

AT LEAST A DOZEN HANDS TOUCH A NORDIC WARE BUNDT PAN BEFORE IT
IS COMPLETE. WE FOLLOW THE PRODUCTION—FROM START TO FINISH—
OF THE ICONIC RIDGED PAN THAT STARTED IT ALL.

An industrial designer digitally sketches a Bundt design. A 3D model of the classic Bundt has all the information needed to create tooling to make the pan.

The pan has a rough perimeter before an automated machine with a high-speed drill bit cuts the metal off.

The drill bit shaves off the rough metal to give it a clean, crisp edge. The leftover aluminum shavings are then recycled.

Bundt pans travel up a conveyor line into a vibratory deburring machine, which is basically a giant rock tumbler.

The vibratory deburring machine tosses the pan around in hundreds of pebbles that vibrate against the pan to create the ideal surface for the nonstick coating to adhere.

The uncoated pan is washed to remove manufacturing oil, metal shavings, and fingerprints. This helps the nonstick coating adhere. From this point on, pans are handled with latex gloves.

A nonstick coating is applied to the exterior of the pan. Then the pan travels down a conveyor belt to the curing oven.

The oven permanently bakes the coating onto the pan. Then the entire coating process is repeated for the inside of the pan.

The pan gets handpacked and labeled. Each packing label includes the phrase "Made in America."

ORIGINAL GERMAN POUND CAKE

Makes 1 (15-cup) Bundt cake

Recipe by Dotty Dalquist

Make one of Dotty Dalquist's favorite Bundt cake recipes inspired by the Nordic Ware pan's European lineage. We made this one in the Anniversary Bundt Pan, a recreation of the original pan Dave designed and their best-selling pan of all time. All ingredients must be at room temperature.

32   whole almonds (34 grams)
1   cup (227 grams) unsalted butter, softened,
     plus more for securing almonds
1   cup (200 grams) granulated sugar
1   cup (120 grams) confectioners' sugar
4   large eggs (200 grams), separated
1   teaspoon (4 grams) vanilla extract
1   teaspoon (4 grams) almond extract
3   cups (375 grams) all-purpose flour, sifted three times
2   teaspoons (10 grams) baking powder
½   teaspoon (1.5 grams) kosher salt
1   cup (240 grams) whole milk, room temperature
Garnish: confectioners' sugar

1. Preheat oven to 350°F (180°C). Spray a 15-cup Bundt pan with baking spray with flour.
2. Place 16 almonds in bottom of prepared pan, securing with a dab of butter. Place another ring of remaining 16 almonds on sides of pan, securing with a dab of butter. Place pan in freezer.
3. In the bowl of a stand mixer fitted with the paddle attachment, beat butter at medium speed until creamy, 3 to 4 minutes.
4. In a small bowl, sift together granulated sugar and confectioners' sugar. Gradually add sugar mixture to butter, beating until fluffy, 3 to 4 minutes, stopping to scrape sides of bowl. Add egg yolks, one at a time, beating until smooth. Beat in extracts.
5. In a medium bowl, sift together flour, baking powder, and salt three times. With mixer on low speed, gradually add flour mixture to butter mixture alternately with milk, beginning and ending with flour mixture, beating just until combined after each addition. Transfer batter to a large bowl; set aside.
6. Clean bowl of stand mixer. Using the whisk attachment, beat egg whites at medium-high speed until stiff peaks form. Fold egg whites into batter. Pour batter into prepared pan.
7. Bake until a wooden pick inserted near center comes out clean, 1 hour to 1 hour and 15 minutes. Let cool in pan for 10 to 15 minutes. Invert cake onto a wire rack, and let cool completely. Garnish with confectioners' sugar, if desired.

BAKE THE BEST BUNDT
OUR TOP TIPS FOR PICKING AND USING YOUR BUNDT PAN

Material and Color Matter. Bundt pans come in glass, stoneware, and silicone, but the best pans are cast aluminum or coated steel. We prefer aluminum because of its even heat conductivity and durability. Light-colored pans lend perfectly baked cakes, while darker surfaces can overly brown crusts.

Ready to Bake. Even with a nonstick surface, it's still a good idea to prepare the inside of your pan. Baking spray with flour works best for Bundts. To avoid overflow in the oven, do not fill the pan more than three-fourths full with batter. Always let your cake cool for 10 to 15 minutes before removing from the pan.

PAN
POWER

A LOOK AT THE MANY NORDIC WARE BUNDT PANS WE USE IN THIS COOKBOOK

You can bake our Bundt recipes with whichever Bundt pan you like—just make sure the cup capacity of the pan you use is the same as the cup capacity called for in the recipe.

BAVARIA BUNDT PAN
Capacity: 10 cups

BRILLIANCE BUNDT PAN
Capacity: 10 cups

ANNIVERSARY BUNDT PAN
Capacity: 15 cups

SWIRL BUNDT PAN
Capacity: 10 cups

ELEGANT PARTY BUNDT PAN
Capacity: 10 cups

6 CUP HERITAGE BUNDT PAN
Capacity: 6 cups

MAGNOLIA BUNDT PAN
Capacity: 10 cups

CHIFFON BUNDT PAN
Capacity: 10 cups

HERITAGE BUNDT PAN
Capacity: 10 cups

KUGELHOPF BUNDT PAN
Capacity: 10 cups

CROWN BUNDT PAN
Capacity: 10 cups

JUBILEE BUNDT PAN
Capacity: 10 cups

FLEUR DE LIS BUNDT PAN
Capacity: 10 cups

ESSENTIAL BUNDT TOOLS

THE KEY EQUIPMENT NEEDED TO MAKE FLAWLESS BUNDTS

NORDIC WARE ULTIMATE BUNDT CLEANING TOOL
This small brush is an excellent way to clean all the nooks and crannies of your Bundt pans without scratching the nonstick coating.

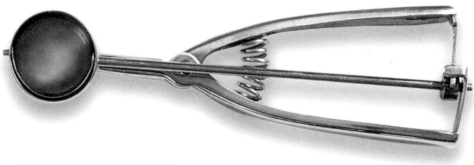

SPRING-LOADED SCOOP
We use a spring-loaded scoop to help scoop alternating batters to create a magical marbled or swirled design with some our recipes.

BALLOON WHISK
Many of our glazes and icings require a quick whisk to bring ingredients together, so a balloon whisk is an essential item to have on hand.

SILICONE SPATULA
A silicone spatula plays a crucial role in smoothing and spreading our Bundt batter into the detailed pans so it bakes into a level, even cake.

SQUEEZE BOTTLE
Small squeeze bottles are a great way to pipe your glazes or icings in a detailed, beautiful way onto your ridged Bundts, particularly those baked in the Brilliance Bundt Pan.

OFFSET SPATULA
An offset spatula has many purposes in the Bundt baker's kitchen, from smoothing the top of the batter before baking to swirling and twirling in fillings.

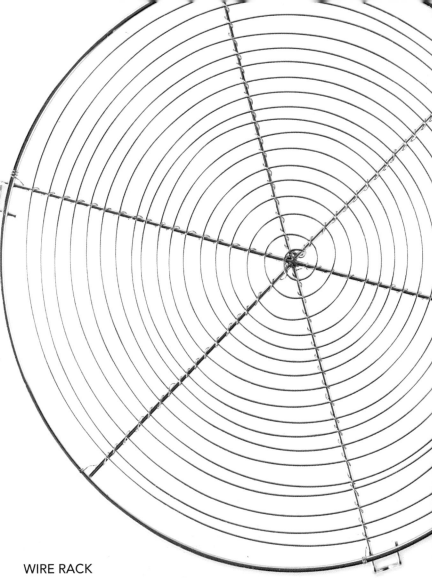

WIRE RACK
Even after removing your cake from the oven, Bundt cakes will continue to cook within their hot pans, so to keep from burning your Bundt cake, always let it cool completely on a wire rack after its initial rest in the pan.

SILICONE PASTRY BRUSH
We use this delicate silicone pastry brush to evenly distribute excess baking spray with flour, keeping it from settling and pooling into the Bundt pan's intricately designed ridges.

SIFTER
We like having a sifter on hand for breaking up clumps in confectioners' sugar and dusting an elegant and sweet coat onto many of our cakes.

CHOCOLATE INDULGENCE

WE KICK OFF OUR BUNDT CAKE
COLLECTION WITH AN ODE
TO ALL THINGS CHOCOLATE,
FEATURING UNADULTERATED
COCOA-RICH CLASSICS,
FROM A CHOCOLATE AND
CARROT CAKE MASH-UP TO
A PEANUT BUTTER- AND
CHOCOLATE-SWIRLED
STUNNER

MEXICAN HOT CHOCOLATE BUNDT CAKE

Makes 1 (10-cup) Bundt cake

Ancho chile gives this chocolate cake a rich heat. Like more spice? Add an extra teaspoon of the ground chile pepper.

1   cup (227 grams) unsalted butter, softened
2   cups (400 grams) granulated sugar
4   large eggs (200 grams), room temperature
1   teaspoon (4 grams) vanilla extract
2¾ cups (344 grams) all-purpose flour
2   teaspoons (4 grams) ground ancho chile pepper
1   teaspoon (5 grams) baking soda
1   teaspoon (3 grams) kosher salt
1½ cups (360 grams) whole milk, room temperature
⅓   cup (25 grams) dark unsweetened cocoa powder
⅓   cup (25 grams) unsweetened cocoa powder
Chocolate Glaze (recipe follows)

1. Preheat oven to 325°F (170°C).
2. In the bowl of a stand mixer fitted with the paddle attachment, beat butter and sugar at medium speed until fluffy, 3 to 4 minutes, stopping to scrape sides of bowl. Add eggs, one at a time, beating well after each addition. Beat in vanilla.
3. In a medium bowl, whisk together flour, ancho chile pepper, baking soda, and salt. With mixer on low speed, gradually add flour mixture to butter mixture alternately with milk, beginning and ending with flour mixture, beating just until combined after each addition. Transfer half of batter to a medium bowl; stir in dark cocoa until smooth. Stir cocoa into remaining batter until smooth.
4. Spray a 10-cup Bundt pan with baking spray with flour. Using 2 (¼-cup) spring-loaded scoops, alternately scoop batters into prepared pan. Tap pan on a kitchen towel-lined counter a few times to settle batter and release any air bubbles.
5. Bake until a wooden pick inserted near center comes out with a few moist crumbs, 45 to 50 minutes. Let cool in pan for 10 minutes. Invert cake onto a wire rack, and let cool completely. Spoon Chocolate Glaze onto cooled cake.

CHOCOLATE GLAZE
Makes ¾ cup

⅔   cup (160 grams) heavy whipping cream
⅔   cup (113 grams) chopped 60% cacao bittersweet chocolate

1. In a small saucepan, heat cream over medium heat, stirring frequently, just until bubbles form around edges of pan. (Do not boil.)
2. In the work bowl of a food processor, place chocolate; process until finely chopped. With processor running, add hot cream in a slow, steady stream until chocolate is melted and mixture is smooth.

PRO TIP
Use 2 (¼-cup) spring-loaded scoops to alternately spoon the regular cocoa and the dark cocoa cake batters into the pan. This will result in a beautiful swirl pattern.

CHOCOLATE-CARROT BUNDT CAKE

Makes 1 (15-cup) Bundt cake

This spin on classic stir-together carrot cake tastes even better the day after it's baked.

1   cup (200 grams) granulated sugar
1   cup (220 grams) firmly packed dark brown sugar
1   cup (224 grams) vegetable oil
4   large eggs (200 grams), room temperature
1   tablespoon (13 grams) vanilla extract
2   cups (250 grams) all-purpose flour
1   tablespoon (6 grams) ground cinnamon
2   teaspoons (10 grams) baking powder
1½ teaspoons (4.5 grams) kosher salt
1   teaspoon (2 grams) ground ginger
½   teaspoon (2.5 grams) baking soda
½   teaspoon (1 gram) ground nutmeg
3   cups (322 grams) lightly packed grated carrot
¾   cup (128 grams) chopped 60% cacao semisweet chocolate
Cream Cheese Glaze (recipe follows)
Garnish: chopped semisweet chocolate

1. Preheat oven to 350°F (180°C).
2. In a large bowl, whisk together sugars, oil, eggs, and vanilla until well combined.
3. In a medium bowl, whisk together flour, cinnamon, baking powder, salt, ginger, baking soda, and nutmeg. Gradually add flour mixture to sugar mixture, whisking just until combined. Fold in carrot and chocolate.
4. Spray a 15-cup Bundt cake pan with baking spray with flour. Pour batter into prepared pan. Tap pan on a kitchen towel-lined counter a few times to settle batter and release any air bubbles.

5. Bake until a wooden pick inserted near center comes out clean, 45 to 50 minutes. Let cool in pan on a wire rack for 15 minutes. Invert cake onto wire rack, and let cool completely. Top with Cream Cheese Glaze. Garnish with chopped chocolate, if desired. Refrigerate until ready to serve.

CREAM CHEESE GLAZE
Makes about 1 cup

8   ounces (226 grams) cream cheese, softened
2   tablespoons (14 grams) confectioners' sugar
2   tablespoons (30 grams) whole milk, room temperature
⅛   teaspoon kosher salt

1. In the bowl of a stand mixer fitted with the paddle attachment, beat cream cheese at medium speed until smooth. Add confectioners' sugar, milk, and salt, beating until well combined and smooth. Use immediately.

Photo by Alison Miksch

PEANUT BUTTER AND CHOCOLATE SWIRL BUNDT CAKE

Makes 1 (10-cup) Bundt cake

A spin on the classic Bundt, this crowd-pleasing cake has swirls of both peanut butter and chocolate batter.

1   cup (227 grams) unsalted butter, softened
1¾ cups (350 grams) granulated sugar
3   large eggs (150 grams), room temperature
2   teaspoons (8 grams) vanilla extract
3   cups (375 grams) bleached self-rising flour
1   teaspoon (3 grams) kosher salt
¾   cup (180 grams) whole buttermilk, room temperature
½   cup (128 grams) creamy peanut butter*
3   tablespoons (15 grams) Dutch process cocoa powder, sifted
1   teaspoon (1 gram) espresso powder
Peanut Butter Frosting (recipe follows)
Garnish: chocolate shavings

1. Preheat oven to 350°F (180°C).
2. In the bowl of a stand mixer fitted with the paddle attachment, beat butter and sugar at medium speed until fluffy, 3 to 4 minutes, stopping to scrape sides of bowl. Add eggs, one at a time, beating well after each addition. Beat in vanilla.
3. In a medium bowl, whisk together flour and salt. In a medium bowl, whisk together buttermilk and peanut butter until well combined. With mixer on low speed, gradually add flour mixture to butter mixture alternately with buttermilk mixture, beginning and ending with flour mixture, beating just until combined after each addition.
4. In a medium bowl, stir together cocoa and espresso powder. Spoon half of batter (about 3 cups [about 682 grams]) onto cocoa mixture, folding until combined.

5. Generously spray a 10-cup Bundt pan with baking spray with flour. Drop heaping tablespoons of each batter into prepared pan, alternating between peanut butter and chocolate batters. Using a knife, swirl batter in a small, circular, looping motion, being careful not to scrape bottom or sides of pan. Tap pan on a kitchen towel-lined counter a few times to settle batter and release any air bubbles.
6. Bake until a wooden pick inserted near center comes out clean, 45 to 50 minutes. Let cool in pan for 30 minutes. Invert cake onto a wire rack, and let cool completely.
7. Transfer cooled cake to a serving plate. Spoon and spread Peanut Butter Frosting onto cake. Garnish with chocolate shavings, if desired.

We used JIF Creamy Peanut Butter.

PEANUT BUTTER FROSTING
Makes about 1 cup

¾   cup (90 grams) confectioners' sugar, sifted
⅓   cup (76 grams) unsalted butter, melted
¼   cup (64 grams) creamy peanut butter

1. In a small bowl, stir together all ingredients until well combined. Use immediately

CHOCOLATE CHIP KUGELHOPF

Makes 1 (10-cup) Bundt cake

Hailing from the Germanic region of Europe, this yeast-leavened cake is known for its signature tall, ringed shape. This recipe replaces the usual raisins with chocolate chips because a little chocolate makes everything better.

2   tablespoons (30 grams) warm water (105°F/41°C to 110°F/43°C)
1½   teaspoons (4.5 grams) active dry yeast
½   cup (113 grams) unsalted butter, softened
½   cup (100 grams) granulated sugar
1   tablespoon (3 grams) orange zest
3   large eggs (150 grams), room temperature
4   cups (500 grams) all-purpose flour
1   teaspoon (3 grams) kosher salt
1   cup (240 grams) whole milk, room temperature
1½   cups (255 grams) 60% cacao semisweet chocolate chips
Garnish: confectioners' sugar, Candied Orange Rind
      (recipe follows)

1. In a small bowl, combine 2 tablespoons (30 grams) warm water and yeast. Let stand until foamy, about 5 minutes.
2. In the bowl of a stand mixer fitted with the paddle attachment, beat butter, granulated sugar, and orange zest at medium speed until creamy, 3 to 4 minutes, stopping to scrape sides of bowl. Add eggs, one at a time, beating well after each addition. Add yeast mixture, beating until combined.
3. In a medium bowl, whisk together flour and salt. With mixer on low speed, gradually add flour mixture to butter mixture alternately with milk, beginning and ending with flour mixture, beating just until combined after each addition. Beat in chocolate chips.

4. Spray a 10-cup Kugelhopf Bundt Pan with baking spray with flour. (See Note.) Spoon batter into prepared pan. Cover with plastic wrap, and let stand in a warm, draft-free place (75°F/24°C) until batter has risen by 1 inch, about 2 hours.
5. Preheat oven to 350°F (180°C).
6. Bake until a wooden pick inserted near center comes out clean, about 30 minutes. Let cool in pan for 10 minutes. Invert cake onto a wire rack, and let cool completely. Garnish with confectioners' sugar and Candied Orange Rind, if desired.

Note: *A regular 10-cup Bundt pan may be substituted.*

Candied Orange Rind

Makes 8 strips

1   navel orange
1⅔   cups (333 grams) granulated sugar, divided
½   cup (120 grams) water

1. Using a channel knife, cut 8 (6-inch) strips of peel from orange. Place strips in a small saucepan; add 1 cup (200 grams) sugar and ½ cup (120 grams) water. Bring to a boil over medium heat; reduce heat, and simmer for 30 minutes. Remove from heat, and let stand for 30 minutes. Remove orange peel, and drain well. Toss peel with remaining ⅔ cup (133 grams) sugar.

CHOCOLATE-COCONUT BUNDT CAKE

Makes 1 (15-cup) Bundt cake

With a hidden tunnel of coconut-chocolate bliss, this decadent Bundt cake packs a welcome surprise with each slice.

1   cup (227 grams) unsalted butter, softened
1½ cups (300 grams) plus 2 tablespoons (24 grams) granulated sugar, divided
3   large eggs (150 grams), room temperature
1   teaspoon (4 grams) plus ½ teaspoon (2 grams) vanilla extract, divided
2   cups (250 grams) plus 2 tablespoons (16 grams) all-purpose flour, divided
¼   cup (21 grams) unsweetened cocoa powder
1   teaspoon (5 grams) baking soda
¾   teaspoon (2.25 grams) plus ⅛ teaspoon kosher salt, divided
½   teaspoon (2.5 grams) baking powder
1   cup (240 grams) plus 3 to 4 tablespoons (45 to 60 grams) coconut milk, divided
1   cup (60 grams) sweetened flaked coconut
1   large egg white (30 grams), room temperature
½   cup (85 grams) 63% cacao dark chocolate chips
1½ cups (180 grams) confectioners' sugar

1. Preheat oven to 350°F (180°C).

2. In the bowl of a stand mixer fitted with the paddle attachment, beat butter and 1½ cups (300 grams) granulated sugar at medium speed until fluffy, 3 to 4 minutes, stopping to scrape sides of bowl. Add eggs, one at a time, beating well after each addition. Beat in 1 teaspoon (4 grams) vanilla.

3. In a medium bowl, whisk together 2 cups (250 grams) flour, cocoa, baking soda, ¾ teaspoon (2.25 grams) salt, and baking powder. With mixer on low speed, gradually add flour mixture to butter mixture alternately with 1 cup (240 grams) coconut milk, beginning and ending with flour mixture, beating just until combined after each addition.

4. In a medium bowl, combine flaked coconut, egg white, remaining 2 tablespoons (24 grams) granulated sugar, remaining 2 tablespoons (16 grams) flour, remaining ½ teaspoon (2 grams) vanilla, and remaining ⅛ teaspoon salt. Stir in chocolate chips.

5. Spray a 15-cup Bundt pan with baking spray with flour. Spoon half of batter into prepared pan. Spoon coconut mixture onto batter, leaving a ¼-inch border around edges of pan. Spoon remaining batter onto coconut mixture. Smooth top with an offset spatula.

6. Bake until a wooden pick inserted near center comes out clean, about 45 minutes. Let cool in pan for 15 minutes. Invert cake onto a wire rack, and let cool completely.

7. In a medium bowl, place confectioners' sugar. Whisk in remaining 3 to 4 tablespoons (45 to 60 grams) coconut milk, 1 tablespoon (15 grams) at a time, until glaze reaches desired consistency. Spoon glaze onto cooled cake. Let stand until glaze is set, about 30 minutes.

PRO TIP
To measure the size of your Bundt pan, count how many cups of water it takes to fill the empty pan to the top. This will allow you to know the true size of the pan so you don't overfill with batter.

Makes 1 (15-cup) Bundt cake

Recipe by Ben Mims

Black cocoa gives this cake a dark richness while white chocolate in the "plain" batter offsets the bitter cocoa with sweetness. Scoop both batters alternately into the Bundt pan using a spring-loaded scoop to create the marbled design without swirling the batters together, or feel free to pour both batters into the pan and swirl the batter with a knife.

2   cups (454 grams) unsalted butter, room temperature and divided
3   cups (600 grams) granulated sugar, divided
4   large egg whites (120 grams), room temperature
3   teaspoons (12 grams) vanilla extract, divided
4   ounces (113 grams) white chocolate, melted
2¼ cups (281 grams) cake flour, divided
2   teaspoons (6 grams) kosher salt, divided
2   large eggs (100 grams), room temperature
4   large egg yolks (74 grams), room temperature
¾   cup (64 grams) black cocoa powder*, sifted
½   cup (120 grams) whole buttermilk, room temperature
Vanilla Bean Glaze (recipe follows)
Black Cocoa Glaze (recipe follows)

1. In the bowl of a stand mixer fitted with the paddle attachment, beat 1 cup (227 grams) butter, and 1½ cups (300 grams) sugar at medium speed until fluffy and pale, 6 to 8 minutes, stopping to scrape sides of bowl. Add egg whites, one at a time, beating well after each addition, about 15 seconds. Beat in 1½ teaspoons (6 grams) vanilla. Scrape bottom and sides of bowl with a rubber spatula. With mixer on medium-high speed, add melted white chocolate, beating until smooth, about 1 minute. Add 1½ cups (187 grams) flour and 1 teaspoon (3 grams) salt, and stir with a rubber spatula just until combined. Transfer white batter to a large bowl, and set aside.
2. Clean bowl of stand mixer and paddle attachment. Return bowl to stand mixer. Using the paddle attachment, beat remaining 1 cup (227 grams) butter, and remaining 1½ cups (300 grams) sugar at medium speed until fluffy and pale, 6 to 8 minutes, stopping to scrape sides of bowl. Add eggs, one at a time, beating well after each addition, about 15 seconds. Add egg yolks, two at a time, beating well after each addition, about 15 seconds. Beat in remaining 1½ teaspoons (6 grams) vanilla. Scrape bottom and sides of bowl with a rubber spatula. Increase mixer speed to medium-high, and beat until smooth, about 1 minute. Add black cocoa, remaining ¾ cup (94 grams) flour, and remaining 1 teaspoon (3 grams) salt, beating until smooth. With mixer on low speed, add buttermilk, beating just until batter comes together. Scrape bottom and sides of bowl with a rubber spatula, and stir just until combined.
3. Spray a 15-cup Bundt pan with baking spray with flour. Using a 2- to 3-ounce spring-loaded scoop, alternately scoop white and black batters into prepared pan. Tap pan on a kitchen towel-lined counter a few times to settle batter and release any air bubbles.
4. Place pan in a cold oven, and bake at 300°F (150°C) until lightly browned on top and a wooden pick inserted near center comes out

BLACK-AND-WHITE CHOCOLATE MARBLE POUND CAKE

clean, 1½ to 2 hours. (See Note.) Let cool in pan for 10 minutes. Invert cake onto a wire rack, and let cool completely.
5. Alternately spoon Vanilla Bean Glaze and Black Cocoa Glaze onto cooled cake, letting each drip down grooves of cake. (Alternatively, pour Black Cocoa Glaze over cake, and let stand until hardened, about 10 minutes. Pour Vanilla Bean Glaze over top, and let stand until hardened, about 10 minutes.)

*Black cocoa is available online or in specialty food stores. Black cocoa is a deeper color than regular cocoa and further alkalized—or "Dutch processed"—to remove virtually all acidity.

Note: *The bake time depends on how long it takes your oven to preheat. Start checking after 1½ hours, and continue baking in 10-minute intervals until cake is done.*

VANILLA BEAN GLAZE
Makes about ½ cup

1   cup (120 grams) confectioners' sugar, sifted
2   tablespoons plus 2 teaspoons (40 grams) heavy whipping cream
½   plump Bourbon-Madagascar vanilla bean, split lengthwise, seeds scraped and reserved
¼   teaspoon kosher salt

1. In a small saucepan, combine confectioners' sugar, cream, vanilla bean and reserved seeds, and salt. Cook over low heat, stirring constantly, until smooth and no lumps remain. Discard vanilla bean. Pour glaze into a bowl, and let cool until it falls off a spoon in a thick, heavy stream.

BLACK COCOA GLAZE
Makes about ½ cup

¾   cup (90 grams) confectioners' sugar, sifted
¼   cup (21 grams) black cocoa powder, sifted
3   tablespoons (45 grams) heavy whipping cream
¼   teaspoon kosher salt

1. In a small saucepan, combine all ingredients. Cook over low heat, stirring constantly, until smooth and no lumps remain. Pour glaze into a bowl, and let cool until it falls off a spoon in a thick, heavy stream.

DOUBLE-CHOCOLATE SPICE BUNDT CAKE

Makes 1 (10-cup) Bundt cake

This chocolate-on-chocolate Bundt gets an undertone of warm, cozy spice from chai tea-infused milk. Just one slice will have the chocolate lover in your life begging for more.

1	cup (240 grams) whole milk, room temperature
2	tea bags (6 grams) chai tea
1	cup (227 grams) unsalted butter, softened
1½	cups (330 grams) firmly packed dark brown sugar
3	large eggs (150 grams), room temperature
1	teaspoon (4 grams) vanilla extract
3	cups (375 grams) all-purpose flour
¾	teaspoon (3.75 grams) baking powder
½	teaspoon (2.5 grams) baking soda
½	teaspoon (1.5 grams) kosher salt
1	cup (240 grams) whole buttermilk, room temperature
1⅓	cups (227 grams) finely chopped 70% cacao dark chocolate
1	cup (170 grams) 60% cacao semisweet chocolate chips, melted and slightly cooled

Bittersweet Chocolate Glaze (recipe follows)

1. Preheat oven to 300°F (150°C).

2. In a small saucepan, heat milk over medium heat just until steaming. (Do not boil.) Remove from heat. Add tea bags; cover and let stand for 10 minutes. Discard tea bags. Reserve ½ cup (120 grams) chai milk for batter and 5 tablespoons (75 grams) chai milk for Bittersweet Chocolate Glaze.

3. In the bowl of a stand mixer fitted with the paddle attachment, beat butter and brown sugar at medium speed until fluffy, 3 to 4 minutes, stopping to scrape sides of bowl. Add eggs, one at a time, beating well after each addition. Beat in vanilla.

4. In a medium bowl, whisk together flour, baking powder, baking soda, and salt. In a small bowl, whisk together buttermilk and reserved ½ cup (120 grams) chai milk. With mixer on low speed, gradually add flour mixture to butter mixture alternately with buttermilk mixture, beginning and ending with flour mixture, beating just until combined after each addition. Beat in chopped chocolate and melted chocolate.

5. Spray a 10-cup Bundt pan with baking spray with flour. Spoon batter into prepared pan, smoothing top with an offset spatula.

6. Bake until a wooden pick inserted near center comes out clean, about 1 hour. Let cool in pan for 10 minutes. Invert cake onto a wire rack, and let cool completely. Drizzle Bittersweet Chocolate Glaze onto cooled cake just before serving.

BITTERSWEET CHOCOLATE GLAZE
Makes about 1 cup

1½	cups (180 grams) confectioners' sugar
½	cup (85 grams) chopped 70% cacao bittersweet chocolate, melted
1	tablespoon (14 grams) unsalted butter, melted
5	tablespoons (75 grams) chai milk, reserved from Double-Chocolate Spice Bundt Cake (recipe precedes)

1. In a medium bowl, whisk together confectioners' sugar, melted chocolate, and melted butter. Add chai milk, 1 tablespoon (15 grams) at a time, whisking until a smooth consistency is reached. Use immediately.

BLACK COCOA BUNDT CAKE

Makes 1 (10-cup) Bundt cake

Black cocoa lends this cake deep chocolate flavor while a Vanilla Bean Glaze imparts an extra note of sweetness and a pop of white.

1¼ cups (284 grams) unsalted butter, softened
2½ cups (500 grams) granulated sugar
4 large eggs (200 grams), room temperature
1½ teaspoons (6 grams) vanilla extract
1½ cups (188 grams) all-purpose flour
⅔ cup (50 grams) black cocoa powder
2½ teaspoons (5 grams) instant espresso powder
1 teaspoon (3 grams) kosher salt
¾ teaspoon (3.75 grams) baking powder
¾ cup (180 grams) whole buttermilk, room temperature
Vanilla Bean Glaze (recipe follows)

1. In the bowl of a stand mixer fitted with the paddle attachment, beat butter and sugar at medium speed until fluffy, 3 to 4 minutes, stopping to scrape sides of bowl. Add eggs, one at a time, beating well after each addition. Beat in vanilla.
2. In a medium bowl, whisk together flour, black cocoa, espresso powder, salt, and baking powder. With mixer on low speed, gradually add flour mixture to butter mixture alternately with buttermilk, beginning and ending with flour mixture, beating just until combined after each addition.
3. Spray a 10-cup Bundt pan with baking spray with flour. Pour batter into prepared pan, smoothing top with a small offset spatula. Tap pan on a kitchen towel-lined counter a few times to settle batter and release any air bubbles.
4. Place pan in a cold oven, and bake at 325°F (170°C) until a wooden pick inserted near center comes out clean, 1 hour to 1 hour and 10 minutes. Let cool in pan for 30 minutes. Invert cake onto a wire rack, and let cool completely.

5. Spoon Vanilla Bean Glaze onto cooled cake, or place Vanilla Bean Glaze in a pastry bag fitted with a medium round tip, and pipe over cake.

Vanilla Bean Glaze

Makes ⅔ cup

1 cup (120 grams) confectioners' sugar
3 tablespoons (45 grams) heavy whipping cream
½ teaspoon (3 grams) vanilla bean paste
½ teaspoon (1.5 grams) kosher salt

1. In a small bowl, stir together all ingredients until smooth. Use immediately

WHAT IS BLACK COCOA?
Ultra-Dutch process cocoa. And what does "ultra-Dutch process" mean? During the Dutch process, cocoa beans are rinsed in an alkaline solution, eliminating the cocoa powder's natural acidity, darkening its hue, and concentrating its flavor. Black cocoa has been Dutched to the most extreme level, creating a product with a pitch-black color and a robust yet smooth cocoa taste. The benefits of baking with black cocoa are twofold, yielding baked goods with incomparable dark cocoa flavor and a velvety black hue.

GERMAN CHOCOLATE CAKE WITH BUTTERSCOTCH GLAZE

Makes 1 (15-cup) Bundt cake

Chock-full of sweet German's chocolate and drizzled with a decadent Butterscotch Glaze, this Bundt cake is an easy and delicious alternative to its more involved layer cake cousin.

¾   cup (64 grams) unsweetened cocoa powder
¾   cup (180 grams) hot brewed coffee
⅓   cup (57 grams) chopped sweetened chocolate baking bar*
½   cup (113 grams) unsalted butter, softened
2   cups (400 grams) granulated sugar
1   tablespoon (13 grams) vanilla extract
3   large egg whites (90 grams), room temperature
3   cups (375 grams) all-purpose flour
1   tablespoon (15 grams) baking powder
1½   teaspoons (4.5 grams) kosher salt
¾   teaspoon (3.75 grams) baking soda
1½   cups (360 grams) whole buttermilk, room temperature
Butterscotch Glaze (recipe follows)

1. Preheat oven to 350°F (180°C).
2. In a medium bowl, whisk together cocoa, coffee, and chocolate until chocolate is melted and mixture is smooth.

3. In the bowl of a stand mixer fitted with the paddle attachment, beat butter, and sugarat medium speed until fluffy, 3 to 4 minutes, stopping to scrape sides of bowl. Add egg whites, one at a time, beating well after each addition. Beat in vanilla. With mixer on low speed, add cocoa mixture, beating until combined.
4. In a medium bowl, whisk together flour, baking powder, salt, and baking soda. Gradually add flour mixture to butter mixture alternately with buttermilk, beginning and ending with flour mixture, beating just until combined after each addition.
5. Spray a 15-cup Bundt pan with baking spray with flour. Pour batter into prepared pan.
6. Bake until a wooden pick inserted near center comes out clean, 45 to 50 minutes. Let cool in pan for 10 minutes. Invert cake onto a wire rack, and let cool completely. Drizzle Butterscotch Glaze onto cooled cake before serving.

*We used Baker's German's Sweet Chocolate Baking Bar.

BUTTERSCOTCH GLAZE
Makes about ¾ cup

1   cup (170 grams) butterscotch chips
⅓   cup (80 grams) half-and-half

1. In a small saucepan, combine butterscotch chips and half-and-half. Cook over medium heat, whisking frequently, until butterscotch is melted and mixture is smooth. Let cool until thickened, about 10 minutes. Use immediately.

ROCKY ROAD BUNDT CAKE

Makes 1 (10-cup) Bundt cake

The ice cream you know and love, now in cake form. This chocolate Bundt cake is brimming with rich pockets of melty chocolate and almonds, all topped with a sweet Marshmallow Glaze.

1   cup (170 grams) chopped 70% cacao bittersweet chocolate baking bars, divided
½   cup (43 grams) Dutch process cocoa powder, sifted
1½   teaspoons (3 grams) espresso powder
½   cup (120 grams) water
⅔   cup (160 grams) sour cream
½   cup (113 grams) unsalted butter, softened
1   cup (220 grams) firmly packed light brown sugar
⅓   cup (67 grams) granulated sugar
3   large eggs (150 grams), room temperature
1   large egg yolk (19 grams), room temperature
1   tablespoon (13 grams) vanilla extract
1   cup (125 grams) plus 2½ tablespoons (20 grams) all-purpose flour, divided
1¼   teaspoons (3.75 grams) kosher salt
¾   teaspoon (3.75 grams) baking soda
⅓   cup (50 grams) chopped toasted almonds
Marshmallow Glaze (recipe follows)
Garnish: marshmallows, sliced toasted almonds, chopped bittersweet chocolate

1. Preheat oven to 325°F (170°C).
2. In a medium bowl, combine ⅔ cup (113 grams) chocolate, cocoa, and espresso powder.
3. In a small saucepan, bring ½ cup (120 grams) water just to a boil over medium-high heat. Pour hot water over chocolate mixture in bowl; let stand for 5 minutes. Whisk until chocolate is melted and mixture is smooth; stir in sour cream until well combined.
4. In the bowl of a stand mixer fitted with the paddle attachment, beat butter and sugars at medium speed until fluffy, about 3 minutes, stopping to scrape sides of bowl. Add eggs and egg yolk, one at a time, beating well after each addition. Beat in vanilla. (Mixture may look slightly curdled at this point, but batter will come together.)

5. In a medium bowl, whisk together 1 cup (125 grams) flour, salt, and baking soda. With mixer on low speed, add flour mixture to butter mixture alternately with chocolate mixture, beginning and ending with flour mixture, beating until combined after each addition and stopping to scrape sides of bowl.
6. In a small bowl, stir together almonds, remaining ⅓ cup (57 grams) chocolate, and remaining 2½ tablespoons (20 grams) flour, stirring until well combined. Fold almond mixture into batter until well combined.
7. Spray a 10-cup Bundt pan with baking spray with flour. Spoon batter into prepared pan. Tap pan on a kitchen towel-lined counter a few times to settle batter and release any air bubbles.
8. Bake until a wooden pick inserted near center comes out clean, 35 to 40 minutes, rotating pan halfway through baking. Let cool in pan for 10 minutes. Using a small offset spatula, gently loosen cake from center of pan. Invert cake onto a wire rack, and let cool completely.
9. Spoon and spread Marshmallow Glaze over top of cooled cake. Garnish with marshmallows, almonds, and chocolate, if desired.

MARSHMALLOW GLAZE
Makes about ½ cup

⅓   cup (30 grams) marshmallow crème*
¼   cup (57 grams) unsalted butter, softened
¼   teaspoon kosher salt
¼   teaspoon (1 gram) vanilla extract
½   cup (60 grams) confectioners' sugar, sifted
2   teaspoons (10 grams) whole milk

1. In the bowl of a stand mixer fitted with the paddle attachment, beat marshmallow crème, butter, salt, and vanilla at medium speed until creamy and well combined, about 2 minutes, stopping to scrape sides of bowl. With mixer on low speed, gradually add confectioners' sugar just until combined. Add milk; beat until smooth and well combined, stopping to scrape sides of bowl. Use immediately.

We used Marshmallow Fluff Original Marshmallow Spread and Crème.

SPIKED WITH SPIRITS

THE DARK 'N STORMY, THE WHITE
RUSSIAN, EGGNOG, AND MORE
GET THEIR BUNDT CAKE DEBUT
IN THIS BEAUTIFULLY
BOOZY CHAPTER

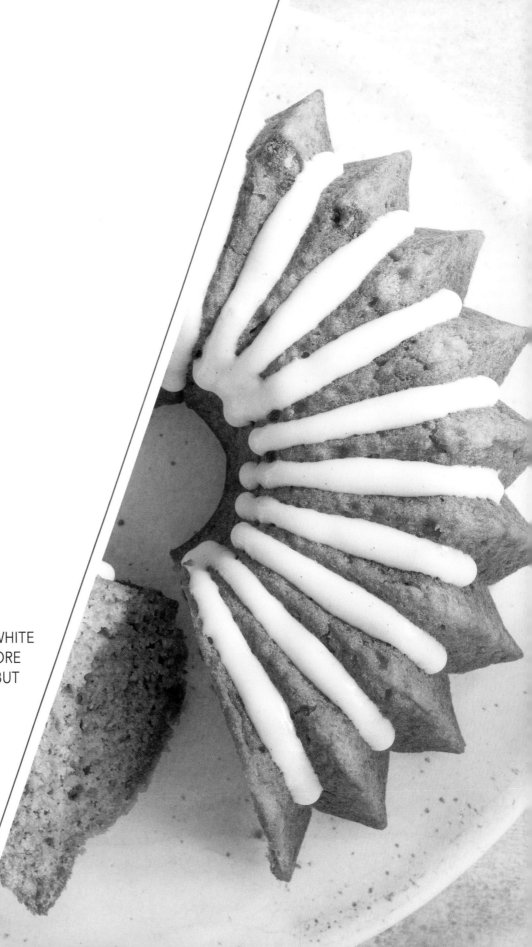

VANILLA BUNDT CAKE WITH BOURBON-VANILLA CARAMEL SAUCE

Makes 1 (15-cup) Bundt cake

Buttery caramel drizzled over a tender vanilla cake—it's a match made in confectionary heaven. With the added hint of bourbon, there's no beating this indulgent treat.

1½ cups (340 grams) unsalted butter, softened
2   cups (400 grams) granulated sugar
1   cup (220 grams) firmly packed dark brown sugar
5   large eggs (250 grams), room temperature
1   tablespoon (13 grams) vanilla extract
3   cups (375 grams) all-purpose flour
1   teaspoon (5 grams) baking powder
½   teaspoon (1.5 grams) kosher salt
1   cup (240 grams) whole milk, room temperature
Bourbon-Vanilla Caramel Sauce (recipe follows)

1. Preheat oven to 325°F (170°C).
2. In the bowl of a stand mixer fitted with the paddle attachment, beat butter and sugars at medium speed until fluffy, 3 to 4 minutes, stopping to scrape sides of bowl. Add eggs, one at a time, beating well after each addition. Beat in vanilla.
3. In a medium bowl, whisk together flour, baking powder, and salt. With mixer on low speed, gradually add flour mixture to butter mixture alternately with milk, beginning and ending with flour mixture, beating just until combined after each addition.

4. Spray a 15-cup Bundt pan with baking spray with flour. Spoon batter into prepared pan.
5. Bake until a wooden pick inserted near center comes out clean, about 1 hour and 5 minutes. Let cool in pan for 10 minutes. Invert cake onto a wire rack, and let cool completely. Drizzle Bourbon-Vanilla Caramel Sauce onto cooled cake just before serving.

BOURBON-VANILLA CARAMEL SAUCE
Makes about 2 cups

2   cups (400 grams) granulated sugar
¼   cup (60 grams) water
½   cup (120 grams) warm heavy whipping cream
     (105°F/41°C to 110°F/43°C)
2   tablespoons (30 grams) bourbon
1   teaspoon (3 grams) kosher salt
½   teaspoon (2 grams) vanilla extract

1. In a medium saucepan, place sugar and ¼ cup (60 grams) water, swirling to combine. Cook over medium-high heat, without stirring, until mixture is amber colored, about 10 minutes. Remove from heat. Carefully stir in warm cream. (Mixture will bubble.) Stir in bourbon, salt, and vanilla. Let cool in pan for 10 minutes, stirring frequently. Transfer to a microwave-safe container. Cover and refrigerate for up to 3 weeks. To serve, heat on high in 30-second intervals, stirring between each, until pourable.

WHITE RUSSIAN BUNDT CAKE

Makes 1 (15-cup) Bundt cake

Recipe by Mandy Dixon

Pastry chef Mandy Dixon and her family serve this moist and flavorful coffee cake at their renowned family-run resort Tutka Bay Lodge in Homer, Alaska. They make a homemade version of coffee liqueur for a fun and easy activity, but name brand Kahlúa is wonderful here as well.

1 cup (227 grams) unsalted butter, softened
1½ cups (300 grams) granulated sugar
4 large eggs (200 grams), room temperature
2 teaspoons (8 grams) vanilla extract
2¾ cups (344 grams) all-purpose flour
1½ teaspoons (7.5 grams) baking powder
1 teaspoon (3 grams) kosher salt
¾ cup (180 grams) heavy whipping cream, room temperature
¼ cup (60 grams) Kahlúa
Kahlúa Pecan Filling (recipe follows)
Kahlúa Glaze (recipe follows)

1. Preheat oven to 325°F (170°C).
2. In the bowl of a stand mixer fitted with the paddle attachment, beat butter and sugar at medium speed until fluffy, 3 to 4 minutes, stopping to scrape sides of bowl. Add eggs, one at a time, beating well after each addition. Beat in vanilla. (Mixture may look slightly curdled at this point, but batter will come together.)
3. In a medium bowl, whisk together flour, baking powder, and salt. In a small bowl, whisk together cream and Kahlúa. With mixer on low speed, gradually add flour mixture to butter mixture alternately with cream mixture, beginning and ending with flour mixture, beating just until combined after each addition.
4. Spray a 15-cup Bundt pan with baking spray with flour. Pour half of batter (2¾ cups [148 grams]) into prepared pan; tap pan on a kitchen towel-lined counter a few times to settle batter and release any air bubbles. Sprinkle with Kahlúa Pecan Filling, leaving a ¼-inch border around edges of pan. (Filling layer will be quite thick). Top with remaining batter. Tap pan on kitchen towel-lined counter a few times to settle batter and release any air bubbles.

5. Bake until a wooden pick inserted near center comes out clean and an instant-read thermometer registers 205°F (96°C), 54 minutes to 1 hour, rotating pan halfway through baking. Let cool in pan for 10 minutes. Invert cake onto a wire rack, and let cool completely. Drizzle Kahlúa Glaze onto cooled cake.

Kahlúa Pecan Filling

Makes about 1 cup

1 cup (113 grams) chopped toasted pecans
½ cup (110 grams) firmly packed light brown sugar
2 tablespoons (30 grams) Kahlúa
1 tablespoon (5 grams) unsweetened cocoa powder
1 teaspoon (2 grams) ground cinnamon

1. In a medium bowl, stir together all ingredients.

Kahlúa Glaze

Makes about 1 cup

1 cup (120 grams) confectioners' sugar, sifted
2 tablespoons (30 grams) heavy whipping cream
2 tablespoons (30 grams) Kahlúa

1. In a small bowl, whisk together all ingredients until smooth. Use immediately.

BROWN SUGAR BUNDT CAKE WITH BOURBON CHERRIES

Makes 1 (10-cup) Bundt cake

This showstopper comes together in a snap. Serve leftover cherries over ice cream or in a cocktail.

¾   cup (170 grams) unsalted butter, softened
1½   cups (330 grams) firmly packed light brown sugar
3   large eggs (150 grams), room temperature
3   cups (375 grams) all-purpose flour
1½   teaspoons (7.5 grams) baking powder
¾   teaspoon (3.75 grams) baking soda
¾   teaspoon (2.25 grams) kosher salt
½   teaspoon (1 gram) ground cinnamon
1¼   cups (300 grams) whole buttermilk, room temperature
1   teaspoon (4 grams) vanilla extract
Bourbon Cherries (recipe follows)

1. Preheat oven to 300°F (150°C).
2. In the bowl of a stand mixer fitted with the paddle attachment, beat butter and brown sugar at medium speed until fluffy, 3 to 4 minutes, stopping to scrape sides of bowl. Add eggs, one at a time, beating well after each addition. Add flour, baking powder, baking soda, salt, and cinnamon, beating just until combined. Beat in buttermilk and vanilla just until combined.
3. Spray a 10-cup Bundt pan with baking spray with flour. Spoon batter into prepared pan, smoothing top with an offset spatula.
4. Bake until a wooden pick inserted near center comes out clean, about 1 hour and 5 minutes. (Cake will rise considerably but will not overflow pan.) Let cool in pan for 10 minutes. Invert cake onto a wire rack, and let cool completely. Spoon Bourbon Cherries over cooled cake, and drizzle with cherry syrup.

BOURBON CHERRIES
Makes about 4 cups

½   cup (100 grams) granulated sugar
½   cup (110 grams) firmly packed light brown sugar
2   cups (480 grams) bourbon
1   pound (454 grams) fresh or thawed frozen pitted cherries*

1. In a small saucepan, combine sugars and bourbon. Cook over medium heat until sugar is dissolved, about 3 minutes. Increase heat to medium-high; cook until thickened and reduced and has the appearance of maple syrup, 20 to 30 minutes. Remove from heat; stir in cherries. Refrigerate in an airtight container for up to 6 weeks.

If using frozen, thaw completely and pat dry.

DARK 'N STORMY BUNDT CAKE

Makes 1 (15-cup) Bundt cake

Inspired by Bermuda's signature Dark 'n Stormy cocktail, this is a classic pound cake with an island update, with dark rum and crystallized ginger added into the batter. A luxurious soak in a rum-spiked glaze ensures that the sugar spirit permeates every bite.

1½   cups (340 grams) unsalted butter, softened
2¾   cups (550 grams) granulated sugar
7   large eggs (350 grams), room temperature
1   tablespoon (3 grams) lime zest
3½   cups (438 grams) all-purpose flour
1   teaspoon (3 grams) kosher salt
¾   cup (180 grams) whole buttermilk, room temperature
½   cup (120 grams) dark rum*
½   cup (88 grams) chopped crystallized ginger
Dark Rum Glaze (recipe follows)

1. Preheat oven to 300°F (150°C).
2. In the bowl of a stand mixer fitted with the paddle attachment, beat butter and sugar at medium speed until fluffy, 6 to 7 minutes, stopping to scrape sides of bowl. Add eggs, one at a time, beating well after each addition. Beat in lime zest. (Mixture may look slightly curdled at this point, but batter will come together.)
3. In a medium bowl, sift together flour and salt. In a small bowl, combine buttermilk and rum. With mixer on low speed, gradually add flour mixture to butter mixture alternately with buttermilk mixture, beginning and ending with flour mixture, beating just until combined after each addition. Fold in ginger.

4. Spray a 15-cup Bundt pan with baking spray with flour. Spoon batter into prepared pan.
5. Bake for 1 hour. Loosely cover with foil, and bake until a wooden pick inserted near center comes out clean, 45 to 55 minutes more. Let cool in pan for 10 minutes. Invert cake onto a wire rack, and let cool completely. Place wire rack over a rimmed baking sheet, and pour Dark Rum Glaze over cooled cake. Let glaze dry before serving.

*We used Gosling's Black Seal Rum.

Dark Rum Glaze

Makes about 1 cup

2¼   cups (270 grams) confectioners' sugar
⅓   cup (80 grams) dark rum

1. In a small bowl, whisk together confectioners' sugar and rum until smooth. Use immediately.

DARK RUM
Distilled from molasses, dark rum (also known as black rum) has a smoky flavor profile similar to whiskey but with a slight sweetness. It shines in recipes that contain molasses, warm spices, or citrus.

ROASTED BANANA RUM BUNDT CAKE

Makes 1 (10-cup) Bundt cake

Ready for a bolder, more sophisticated take on simple banana bread? Time to bring out the Bundt pan. This recipe uses roasted bananas and tangy buttermilk to create an extra-smooth, stir-together batter and tender crumb that translate beautifully to cake form. Buttery spiced rum paired with the gooey Roasted Bananas equals pure indulgence.

Roasted Bananas (recipe follows)
1   ripe banana (124 grams), mashed
⅔   cup (160 grams) whole buttermilk, room temperature
1   cup (220 grams) firmly packed dark brown sugar
½   cup (112 grams) canola oil
¼   cup (60 grams) dark rum
2   large eggs (100 grams), room temperature
1   teaspoon (4 grams) vanilla extract
2½   cups (312 grams) cake flour
1   teaspoon (5 grams) baking soda
1   teaspoon (5 grams) baking powder
½   teaspoon (1.5 grams) kosher salt
Vanilla Cream Cheese Glaze (recipe follows)

1. Preheat oven to 325°F (170°C).
2. In the work bowl of a food processor, place Roasted Bananas, mashed banana, and buttermilk; process until smooth. Transfer to a large bowl; whisk in brown sugar, oil, rum, eggs, and vanilla.
3. In a medium bowl, whisk together flour, baking soda, baking powder, and salt. Fold flour mixture into banana mixture just until combined.
4. Spray a 10-cup Bundt pan with baking spray with flour. Spoon batter into prepared pan. Tap pan on a kitchen towel-lined counter a few times to settle batter and release any air bubbles.
5. Bake until a wooden pick inserted near center comes out clean, 40 to 45 minutes. Let cool in pan for 10 minutes. Invert cake onto a wire rack, and let cool completely. Spoon or pipe Vanilla Cream Cheese Glaze onto cooled cake.

ROASTED BANANAS

Makes 3 bananas

3   medium unpeeled bananas (672 grams)

1. Preheat oven to 400°F (200°C).
2. On a baking sheet, place unpeeled bananas.
3. Bake until completely black, 20 to 25 minutes. Let cool completely; peel bananas.

VANILLA CREAM CHEESE GLAZE

Makes ½ cup

¼   cup (56 grams) cream cheese, softened
½   cup (60 grams) confectioners' sugar
1   tablespoon (15 grams) whole milk
1   tablespoon (15 grams) dark rum
¼   teaspoon (1.5 grams) vanilla bean paste

1. In the bowl of a stand mixer fitted with the paddle attachment, beat cream cheese at medium speed until smooth. With mixer on low speed, gradually add confectioners' sugar, beating until combined. Add milk, rum, and vanilla bean paste, beating until smooth. Use immediately.

PRO TIP
After coating the pan with baking spray with flour, use a pastry brush to evenly spread any excess spray. This allows the batter to fully fill the pan's grooves, resulting in a sharper showstopping design once the cake is baked.

VANILLA SYRUP
Made of simple syrup imbued with vanilla bean seeds, vanilla syrup is delicious as a soak for a cake, added to frosting, or simply splashed in your coffee. While it may be found in some specialty stores, it is widely available online through producers like Heilala Vanilla.

VANILLA SAVARIN

Makes 1 (10-cup) Bundt cake

This Old-World French dessert is a delicious fusion of buttery cake and yeasted bread. Though it's traditionally soaked in orange liqueur, this cake is soaked in a blend of vanilla syrup and spiced rum and piled high with Spiced Vanilla Chantilly Crème for an island twist.

¼ cup (50 grams) granulated sugar
1 vanilla bean, split lengthwise, seeds scraped and reserved
2⅔ cups (333 grams) all-purpose flour
1 tablespoon (9 grams) instant yeast
4 large eggs (200 grams), room temperature
¼ cup (60 grams) warm whole milk (105°F/41°C to 110°F/43°C)
1½ teaspoons (6 grams) vanilla extract
1 teaspoon (3 grams) kosher salt
¾ cup (170 grams) unsalted butter, room temperature (see Note)
Vanilla Rum Syrup (recipe follows)
Spiced Vanilla Chantilly Crème (recipe follows)
Garnish: sliced fresh strawberries

1. In a spice grinder or the work bowl of a small food processor, place sugar and reserved vanilla bean seeds; pulse until combined. Transfer vanilla sugar to a medium bowl; add flour and yeast, stirring to combine.
2. In the bowl of a stand mixer fitted with the paddle attachment, whisk together eggs, warm milk, vanilla extract, and salt by hand. With mixer on medium speed, gradually add sugar mixture, beating until a thick, sticky dough forms, about 1 minute. Gradually add butter, beating until combined. Increase mixer speed to high, and beat until dough is smooth and elastic and pulls away from sides of bowl but not bottom, about 4 minutes. Cover and let rise in a warm, draft-free place (75°F/24°C) until doubled in size, about 1 hour.
3. Spray a 10-cup Bundt pan with baking spray with flour. Gently punch down dough, and place in prepared pan. Using floured hands, press dough until it is even and fills ridges of pan. (The dough will feel very thick and sticky.) Tap pan on a kitchen towel-lined counter a few times to settle dough and release any air bubbles. Cover and let rise in a warm, draft-free place (75°F/24°C) until pan is three-fourths full, about 30 minutes.
4. Preheat oven to 350°F (180°C).
5. Bake until golden and an instant-read thermometer inserted near center registers 190°F (88°C), about 25 minutes. Let cool in pan for 10 minutes. Trim cake to level, if necessary. Invert cake onto a wire rack. Pour half of Vanilla Rum Syrup in pan, and place cake back in pan. Pour remaining Vanilla Rum Syrup over cake; let stand for 5 minutes. Invert cake onto a rimmed dish, letting excess syrup drain. Transfer cake to a serving dish. Pipe Spiced Vanilla Chantilly Crème into center of cake. Garnish with strawberries, if desired.

Note: *It is important for the butter to be room temperature, not just softened, so it can be incorporated into the dough faster. If you need to get your butter to room temperature quickly, microwave it in 5-second intervals until it reaches the proper consistency. Try not to melt it.*

VANILLA RUM SYRUP
Makes about 2¾ cups

1 cup (200 grams) granulated sugar
½ cup (120 grams) water
1⅓ cups (400 grams) vanilla syrup
¼ cup plus 3 tablespoons (105 grams) spiced rum

1. In a small saucepan, bring sugar and ½ cup (120 grams) water to a boil over medium-high heat, stirring occasionally, until sugar dissolves. Remove from heat; stir in vanilla syrup and rum. Let cool slightly.

SPICED VANILLA CHANTILLY CRÈME
Makes about 3 cups

1½ cups (360 grams) cold heavy whipping cream
2 teaspoons (10 grams) spiced rum
½ vanilla bean, split lengthwise, seeds scraped and reserved
¼ cup plus 1 tablespoon (37 grams) confectioners' sugar

1. In the bowl of a stand mixer fitted with the paddle attachment, combine cold cream, rum, and reserved vanilla bean seeds. With mixer on high speed, gradually add confectioners' sugar, beating until stiff peaks form. Cover and refrigerate until ready to serve.

RUM RAISIN BUNDT CAKE

Makes 1 (15-cup) Bundt cake

This extravagant Bundt cake makes the most of the classic combination of buttery rum and sunny-sweet raisins.

1	cup (234 grams) dark spiced rum
¾	cup (120 grams) packed golden raisins
½	cup (80 grams) packed raisins
1	cup (227 grams) unsalted butter, softened
1	cup (200 grams) granulated sugar
⅓	cup (73 grams) firmly packed light brown sugar
2½	teaspoons (10 grams) firmly packed orange zest
4	large eggs (200 grams), room temperature
1½	teaspoons (9 grams) vanilla bean paste
3⅔	cups (458 grams) all-purpose flour
3½	teaspoons (17.5 grams) baking powder
1¼	teaspoons (3.75 grams) kosher salt
¾	teaspoon (1.5 gram) ground cinnamon
¼	teaspoon ground cardamom
1⅓	cups (320 grams) whole milk, room temperature

Spiced Rum Glaze (recipe follows)

1. In a small saucepan, bring rum just to a boil over medium-high heat. Remove from heat; stir in raisins. Cover and let stand for 30 minutes, stirring occasionally. Drain raisins, reserving rum.

2. Preheat oven to 325°F (170°C).

3. In the bowl of a stand mixer fitted with the paddle attachment, beat butter, sugars, and orange zest at medium speed until fluffy, about 3 minutes, stopping to scrape sides of bowl. Add eggs, one at a time, beating until well combined after each addition. Beat in vanilla bean paste. (Mixture may look slightly curdled at this point, but batter will come together.)

4. In a medium bowl, whisk together flour, baking powder, salt, cinnamon, and cardamom. In a medium bowl, whisk together milk and 2 tablespoons (28 grams) reserved rum. With mixer on low speed, add flour mixture to butter mixture alternately with milk mixture, beginning and ending with flour mixture, beating until combined after each addition and stopping to scrape sides of bowl.

5. Reserve ¼ cup (58 grams) drained raisins for topping; fold remaining raisins into batter.

6. Spray a 15-cup Bundt pan with baking spray with flour. Spoon batter into prepared pan. Tap pan on a kitchen towel-lined counter a few times to settle batter and release any air bubbles.

7. Bake until a wooden pick inserted near center comes out clean and an instant-read thermometer registers 205°F (96°C), 55 minutes to 1 hour. Let cool in pan for 10 minutes. Invert cake onto a wire rack placed over a rimmed baking sheet; brush all over with remaining reserved rum, and let cool completely. Spoon Spiced Rum Glaze onto cooled cake. Garnish with remaining drained raisins.

SPICED RUM GLAZE
Makes about ⅔ cup

1½	cups (180 grams) confectioners' sugar, sifted
1½	tablespoons (21 grams) dark spiced rum
1	tablespoon (15 grams) whole milk
1	tablespoon (14 grams) unsalted butter, melted
¼	teaspoon (0.75 grams) kosher salt

1. In a medium bowl, stir together all ingredients until smooth. Use immediately.

EGGNOG BUNDT CAKE

Makes 1 (10-cup) Bundt cake

This Eggnog Bundt Cake doubles down on the rum flavor with extract and a creamy dose of eggnog stirred right into the batter. Topped with a buttery Rum Glaze, it's the perfect accompaniment to holiday celebrations.

¾   cup (170 grams) unsalted butter, softened
1¼ cups (250 grams) granulated sugar
¼   cup (55 grams) firmly packed light brown sugar
3   large eggs (150 grams), room temperature
1½ teaspoons (6 grams) rum extract
2½ cups (313 grams) all-purpose flour
1¾ teaspoons (8.75 grams) baking powder
1¼ teaspoons (2 grams) ground nutmeg
1   teaspoon (3 grams) kosher salt
½   teaspoon (2.5 grams) baking soda
½   teaspoon (1 gram) ground cinnamon
¾   cup (180 grams) eggnog, room temperature
½   cup (120 grams) whole milk, room temperature
Rum Glaze (recipe follows)

1. Preheat oven to 325°F (170°C).

2. In a large bowl, beat butter and sugars with a mixer at medium speed until fluffy, 3 to 4 minutes, stopping to scrape sides of bowl. Add eggs, one at a time, beating well after each addition. Beat in rum extract.

3. In a medium bowl, whisk together flour, baking powder, nutmeg, salt, baking soda, and cinnamon. In a small bowl, stir together eggnog and milk. With mixer on low speed, gradually add flour mixture to butter mixture alternately with eggnog mixture, beginning and ending with flour mixture, beating just until combined after each addition.

4. Spray a 10-cup Bundt pan with baking spray with flour. Spoon batter into prepared pan.

5. Bake until a wooden pick inserted near center comes out clean, 45 to 55 minutes. Let cool in pan for 15 minutes. Invert cake onto a wire rack, and let cool completely. Drizzle Rum Glaze onto cooled cake. Store in an airtight container for up to 3 days.

RUM GLAZE

Makes ¾ cup

2   cups (240 grams) confectioners' sugar
¼   teaspoon (1 gram) rum extract
3   tablespoons (45 grams) whole milk

1. In a medium bowl, whisk together confectioners' sugar and rum extract. Add milk, 1 tablespoon (15 grams) at a time, whisking until a pourable consistency is reached.

FRUITCAKE BUNDT

Makes 1 (15-cup) Bundt cake

The yuletide favorite was destined to be transformed into a beautiful Bundt. Packed with pecans and brandy-soaked fruit, this cake makes decking the halls all the easier.

1   (16-ounce) container (453 grams) mixed candied fruit
1   cup (240 grams) brandy
½   cup (94 grams) lightly packed dried cherries
½   cup (90 grams) lightly packed golden raisins
1   cup (227 grams) unsalted butter, softened
2   cups (400 grams) granulated sugar
4   large eggs (200 grams), room temperature
1½   teaspoons (6 grams) vanilla extract
2¼   cups (254 grams) pecan halves
1¾   cups (219 grams) all-purpose flour
2   teaspoons (10 grams) baking powder
1   teaspoon (3 grams) kosher salt
½   cup (120 grams) whole buttermilk, room temperature
Garnish: confectioners' sugar

1. In a large microwave-safe bowl, combine candied fruit, brandy, raisins, and cranberries. Heat on high until hot, 2 to 3 minutes. Let stand for at least 1 hour, stirring occasionally.
2. Preheat oven to 325°F (170°C).
3. In the bowl of a stand mixer fitted with the paddle attachment, beat butter and granulated sugar at medium speed until fluffy, 3 to 4 minutes, stopping to scrape sides of bowl. Add eggs, one at a time, beating well after each addition. Beat in vanilla.

4. In the work bowl of a food processor, pulse pecans until finely ground. (Do not overprocess.) Transfer to a medium bowl, and whisk in flour, baking powder, and salt. With mixer on low speed, gradually add pecan mixture to butter mixture alternately with buttermilk, beginning and ending with pecan mixture, beating just until combined after each addition. Strain soaked fruit, and fold into batter. (Discard strained brandy or reserve for another use.)
5. Spray a 15-cup Bundt pan with baking spray with flour. Spoon batter into prepared pan. Tap pan on a kitchen towel-lined counter a few times to settle batter and release any air bubbles.
6. Bake until a wooden pick inserted near center comes out clean and an instant-read thermometer registers 205°F (96°C), 1 hour and 15 minutes to 1½ hours, loosely covering with foil halfway through baking to prevent excess browning. Let cool in pan for 15 minutes. Using a small offset spatula, gently loosen center and edges of cake. Invert cake onto a wire rack, and let cool completely. Garnish with confectioners' sugar, if desired.

PRO TIP
Feel free to use any combination of dried fruit in this recipe. Dried cherries, currants, or chopped, dried apricots would work well in this cake.

BROWN SUGAR-BOURBON POUND CAKE

Makes 1 (15-cup) Bundt cake

Golden with brown sugar and bourbon, this aromatic pound cake offers simple perfection. Finish off this cake with a generous pour of caramel sauce and a scattering of candied pecans for a satisfying crunch.

1	cup (227 grams) unsalted butter, softened
1½	cups (330 grams) firmly packed light brown sugar
½	cup (100 grams) granulated sugar
½	teaspoon packed orange zest
4	large eggs (200 grams), room temperature
2	teaspoona (8 grams) vanilla extract
2⅔	cups (333 grams) all-purpose flour
1	teaspoon (3 grams) kosher salt
½	teaspoon (1 gram) ground cinnamon
¼	teaspoon (1.25 grams) baking soda
⅔	cup (160 grams) whole buttermilk, room temperature
¼	cup (60 grams) bourbon

Bourbon Caramel Sauce (recipe follows)
Garnish: chopped candied pecans

1. Preheat oven to 325°F (170°C).
2. In the bowl of a stand mixer fitted with the paddle attachment, beat butter, sugars, and orange zest at medium speed until fluffy, 3 to 4 minutes, stopping to scrape sides of bowl. Add eggs, one at a time, beating well after each addition. Beat in vanilla.
3. In a medium bowl, whisk together flour, salt, cinnamon, and baking soda. In a small bowl, whisk together buttermilk and bourbon. With mixer on low speed, gradually add flour mixture to butter mixture alternately with buttermilk mixture, beginning and ending with flour mixture, beating just until combined after each addition.

4. Generously spray (see Note) a 15-cup Bundt pan with baking spray with flour. Spoon batter into prepared pan. Tap pan on a kitchen towel-lined counter a few times to settle batter and release any air bubbles.
5. Bake until a wooden pick inserted near center comes out clean, about 1 hour. Let cool in pan for 30 minutes. Invert cake onto a wire rack, and let cool completely.
6. Transfer cake to a serving plate; drizzle Bourbon Caramel Sauce onto cooled cake. Garnish with candied pecans, if desired. Serve with any additional sauce.

Note: *The large amount of brown sugar in this cake gives it a softer texture, making it more likely to stick to the pan and tear when inverting after baking. Make sure you spray your pan generously so you get a clean release.*

BOURBON CARAMEL SAUCE
Makes about ¾ cup

½	cup (110 grams) firmly packed light brown sugar
⅓	cup (113 grams) dark corn syrup
2½	tablespoons (37.5 grams) whole buttermilk
2	tablespoons (28 grams) unsalted butter, cubed and softened
¼	teaspoon kosher salt
1½	teaspoons (7.5 grams) bourbon
¼	teaspoon (1 gram) vanilla extract

1. In a medium saucepan, combine brown sugar, corn syrup, buttermilk, butter, and salt. Bring to a boil over medium-high heat; cook, whisking constantly, for 2 minutes. Remove from heat; whisk in bourbon and vanilla. Transfer mixture to a medium microwave-safe bowl; let cool for 20 minutes before using.

Note: *If sauce begins to set up, microwave on high in 10-second intervals, stirring between each, until melted and smooth. Let cool to desired consistency.*

BEAUMES-DE-VENISE BUNDT CAKE WITH APRICOTS

Makes 1 (10-cup) Bundt cake

I couldn't resist twirling up one of our favorite classic French cakes, named after a town in the Vaucluse and the sweet, fortified wine produced there. The recipe traditionally calls for Beaumes-de-Venise wine, but I love the taste of Chablis. Any inexpensive muscat or Sauternes will do as well.

1½	cups (360 grams) Chablis
2	cups (256 grams) chopped dried apricots
1	cup (227 grams) plus 4 tablespoons (56 grams) unsalted butter, softened and divided
¼	cup (56 grams) extra-virgin olive oil
1¾	cups (350 grams) plus 3 tablespoons (36 grams) granulated sugar, divided
2	teaspoons (4 grams) tightly packed lemon zest
2	teaspoons (4 grams) tightly packed orange zest
2	teaspoons (8 grams) vanilla extract
4	large eggs (200 grams), room temperature
3½	cups (438 grams) all-purpose flour
2	teaspoons (10 grams) baking powder
2	teaspoons (6 grams) kosher salt

1. In a small saucepan, bring Chablis to a gentle boil over medium heat. Add apricots, and remove from heat. Let stand until cool, about 30 minutes.

2. Preheat oven to 325°F (170°C).

3. In the bowl of a stand mixer fitted with the paddle attachment, beat 1 cup (227 grams) butter and oil at medium speed for 5 to 10 seconds. Add 1½ cups (300 grams) sugar, lemon zest, orange zest, and vanilla; beat until fluffy, 3 to 4 minutes. Add eggs, one at time, beating well after each addition.

4. In a medium bowl, whisk together flour, baking powder, and salt. With mixer on low speed, gradually add flour mixture to butter mixture alternately with Chablis mixture, beginning and ending with flour mixture, beating just until combined after each addition.

5. Brush a 10-cup Bundt pan with 2 tablespoons (28 grams) butter, coating inside pan, and sprinkle with 3 tablespoons (36 grams) sugar; shake pan to make sure pan is coated with sugar, lightly tapping to get rid of excess. Spoon batter into prepared pan, smoothing top with a small offset spatula.

6. Bake until golden brown and a wooden pick inserted near center comes out clean, 1 hour and 20 minutes to 1½ hours, covering with foil after 45 minutes of baking to prevent excess browning. Let cool in pan for 15 minutes. Invert cake onto a wire rack, and brush with remaining 2 tablespoons (28 grams) softened butter; immediately sprinkle with remaining ¼ cup (50 grams) sugar. Serve warm or at room temperature.

CHERRIES JUBILEE BUNDT CAKE

Makes 1 (10-cup) Bundt cake

Cherries jubilee is a classic dessert sauce, featuring a combo of cherries and liqueur that is then flambéed and served over heaping scoops of ice cream. This Bundt cake take provides all the original delights, now offered by the slice.

¾   cup (170 grams) unsalted butter, softened
1½   cups (300 grams) granulated sugar, divided
¼   cup (55 grams) firmly packed light brown sugar
½   teaspoon (2 grams) firmly packed orange zest
3   large eggs (150 grams), room temperature
1½   teaspoons (9 grams) vanilla bean paste, divided
½   teaspoon (2 grams) almond extract
2½   cups (313 grams) all-purpose flour
2½   teaspoons (12.5 grams) baking powder
1   teaspoon (3 grams) kosher salt
¾   cup (180 grams) whole buttermilk, room temperature
3   tablespoons (39 grams) brandy, divided
2   cups (265 grams) fresh or 2 cups (380 grams) frozen halved pitted sweet cherries (see Notes)
½   cup (120 grams) water
Vanilla Bean-Brandy Glaze (recipe follows)
Garnish: fresh cherries

1. Preheat oven to 325°F (170°C).
2. In the bowl of a stand mixer fitted with the paddle attachment, beat butter, 1¼ cups (250 grams) granulated sugar, brown sugar, and orange zest at medium speed until fluffy, 3 to 4 minutes, stopping to scrape sides of bowl. Add eggs, one at a time, beating well after each addition. Beat in 1 teaspoon (6 grams) vanilla bean paste and almond extract.
3. In a medium bowl, whisk together flour, baking powder, and salt. In a small bowl, whisk together buttermilk and 1 tablespoon

(13 grams) brandy. With mixer on low speed, gradually add flour mixture to butter mixture alternately with buttermilk mixture, beginning and ending with flour mixture, beating just until combined after each addition. Fold in cherries. (It's OK if cherries tint batter; this will go away after baking.)
4. Spray a 10-cup Bundt pan with baking spray with flour. Spoon batter into prepared pan. Tap pan on a kitchen towel-lined counter a few times to settle batter and release any air bubbles.
5. Bake until a wooden pick inserted near center comes out clean and an instant-read thermometer registers 205°F (96°C), 50 to 55 minutes. Let cool in pan for 15 minutes. Invert cake onto a wire rack placed over a rimmed baking sheet.
6. Meanwhile, in a medium saucepan, combine ½ cup (120 grams) water and remaining ¼ cup (50 grams) granulated sugar. Bring to a boil over medium-high heat; cook, stirring frequently, until sugar dissolves. Remove from heat; stir in remaining 2 tablespoons (26 grams) brandy and remaining ½ teaspoon (3 grams) vanilla bean paste. Let cool for 5 minutes; brush all over warm cake. Let cake cool completely.
7. Using a small spoon, drizzle Vanilla Bean-Brandy Glaze into and over grooves of cooled cake. Garnish with cherries, if desired.

Notes: *If using frozen cherries, be sure to thaw, drain, and thoroughly pat cherries dry before measuring and using in this recipe. To help keep cake level and stable while baking, place an oven-safe cooling rack directly on your oven rack to create a sturdy, metal, cross-hatched surface to rest Bundt pan on.*

VANILLA BEAN-BRANDY GLAZE
Makes ⅔ cup

1½   cups (180 grams) confectioners' sugar, sifted
3   tablespoons (39 grams) brandy
1   teaspoon (6 grams) vanilla bean paste
¼   teaspoon kosher salt

1. In a small bowl, stir together all ingredients until smooth and well combined. Use immediately.

PRO TIP
Firmly tapping the pan on the counter several times helps to rid batter of any unwanted air pockets and moves batter into the Bundt pan's grooves.

FABULOUS & FRUITY

JUICY STONE FRUIT, CRUNCHY APPLES, PLUMP BERRIES, AND BRIGHT CITRUS PLAY INTEGRAL ROLES IN EACH OF THESE FRESH FRUIT-FILLED BUNDT CAKES

ALMOND-STRAWBERRY BUNDT CAKE

Makes 1 (10-cup) Bundt cake

Sprinkling the bottom and sides of the Bundt pan with sliced almonds before adding the batter gives this cake a lovely crunchy crust and beautiful sides.

¾   cup (170 grams) unsalted butter, softened
2   cups (400 grams) granulated sugar
3   large eggs (150 grams), room temperature
½   teaspoon (2 grams) almond extract
2¼   cups (281 grams) all-purpose flour
⅔   cup (64 grams) super-fine blanched almond flour*
1   tablespoon (15 grams) baking powder
¾   teaspoon (2.25 grams) kosher salt
1¼   cups (300 grams) whole buttermilk, room temperature
1   cup (170 grams) ¼-inch-diced fresh strawberries
⅓   cup (38 grams) sliced almonds
Garnish: confectioners' sugar

1. Preheat oven to 325°F (170°C).
2. In the bowl of a stand mixer fitted with the paddle attachment, beat butter and granulated sugar at medium speed until fluffy, 3 to 4 minutes, stopping to scrape sides of bowl. Add eggs, one at a time, beating well after each addition. Beat in almond extract.
3. Using a fine-mesh sieve, sift together flours and baking powder into a medium bowl; whisk in salt. With mixer on low speed, gradually add flour mixture to butter mixture alternately with buttermilk, beginning and ending with flour mixture, beating just until combined after each addition; fold in strawberries.

4. Spray a 10-cup Bundt pan with baking spray with flour. Sprinkle sliced almonds in bottom and on sides of pan. Spoon batter into prepared pan, smoothing top. Tap pan on a kitchen towel-lined counter a few times to settle batter and release any air bubbles. (Pan will be quite full, but batter will not overflow during baking.)
5. Bake until a wooden pick inserted near center comes out clean, 45 to 55 minutes, loosely covering with foil during last 15 minutes of baking to prevent excess browning. Let cool in pan for 15 minutes. Invert cake onto wire rack, and let cool completely. Garnish with confectioners' sugar before serving, if desired.

We used Bob's Red Mill Super-Fine Almond Flour.

Photo by Alison Miksch

PEACH AND CARDAMOM BUNDT CAKE

Makes 1 (10-cup) Bundt cake

Packed with chopped fresh peaches, this spiced Bundt cake has delicious pockets of juicy sweetness in every bite.

1	cup (227 grams) unsalted butter, softened
1½	cups (300 grams) granulated sugar
3	large eggs (150 grams), room temperature
1	teaspoon (4 grams) vanilla extract
¼	teaspoon (1 gram) almond extract
3	cups (375 grams) all-purpose flour
1	teaspoon (5 grams) baking powder
1	teaspoon (2 grams) ground cardamom
½	teaspoon (1.5 grams) kosher salt
½	cup (120 grams) whole buttermilk, room temperature
1½	cups (300 grams) chopped peeled fresh peaches
	Crème Fraîche Glaze (recipe follows)

1. Preheat oven to 325° (170°C).
2. In the bowl of a stand mixer fitted with the paddle attachment, beat butter and sugar at medium speed until fluffy, 3 to 4 minutes, stopping to scrape sides of bowl. Add eggs, one at a time, beating just until combined after each addition. Beat in extracts.
3. In a medium bowl, whisk together flour, baking powder, cardamom, and salt. With mixer on low speed, gradually add flour mixture to butter mixture alternately with buttermilk, beginning and ending with flour mixture, beating just until combined after each addition. Stir in peaches.
4. Spray a 10-cup Bundt pan with baking spray with flour. Spoon batter into prepared pan, smoothing top with an offset spatula.
5. Bake until a wooden pick inserted near center comes out clean, 1 hour and 10 minutes to 1 hour and 15 minutes. Let cool in pan on a wire rack for 10 minutes. Invert cake onto wire rack, and let cool completely. Drizzle Crème Fraîche Glaze onto cooled cake.

CRÈME FRAÎCHE GLAZE

Makes about ⅓ cup

1	cup (120 grams) confectioners' sugar
2	tablespoons (30 grams) crème fraîche
1	tablespoon (15 grams) warm water

1. Whisk together confectioners' sugar, crème fraîche, and 1 tablespoon (15 grams) warm water until smooth. Use immediately.

PRO TIP
If you have difficulty locating whole buttermilk, you can make a quickly make your own. Simply add 1 tablespoon (15 grams) distilled white vinegar or lemon juice to 1 cup (240 grams) whole milk. Let stand for 5 minutes to allow mixture to thicken.

CRANBERRY STREUSEL BUNDT CAKE

Makes 1 (10-cup) Bundt cake

Recipe by Rebecca Firth

The tartness of cranberries, ribbons of streusel, and rich, buttery crumb coupled with the fresh nutmeg and fragrant five-spice blend take this cake to the next level. Fresh cranberries are ideal, but frozen will work in a pinch. If using frozen, don't thaw them before folding into the batter.

1½ cups (300 grams) granulated sugar
4 large eggs (200 grams), room temperature
1 large egg yolk (19 grams), room temperature
1½ cups (360 grams) sour cream, room temperature
¾ cup (168 grams) vegetable oil
1½ tablespoons (9 grams) tightly packed orange zest
1½ tablespoons (19.5 grams) vanilla extract
2⅔ cups (333 grams) all-purpose flour
1 tablespoon (15 grams) baking powder
1½ teaspoons (3 grams) ground cinnamon
1 teaspoon (2 grams) Chinese five-spice powder
¾ teaspoon (2.25 grams) kosher salt
½ teaspoon grated fresh nutmeg
½ cup (120 grams) whole milk, room temperature
2¼ cups (382.5 grams) fresh or frozen cranberries
Spiced Streusel (recipe follows)
Citrus Glaze (recipe follows)
Garnish: Cranberry Powder (recipe follows)

1. Preheat oven to 350°F (180°C).
2. In the bowl of a stand mixer fitted with the paddle attachment, beat sugar, eggs, and egg yolk at medium speed until light and fluffy, about 4 minutes, stopping to scrape sides of bowl. With mixer on low speed, add sour cream, oil, orange zest, and vanilla. Increase mixer speed to medium, and beat until combined.
3. In a medium bowl, whisk together flour, baking powder, cinnamon, five-spice powder, salt, and nutmeg. With mixer on low speed, gradually add flour mixture to sugar mixture alternately with milk, beginning and ending with flour mixture, beating just until combined after each addition. Fold in cranberries.
4. Spray a 10-cup Bundt pan with baking spray with flour. Pour one-third of batter into prepared pan. Sprinkle with half of Spiced

Streusel. Add another one-third of batter, and sprinkle with remaining Spiced Streusel. Pour remaining batter on top, using an offset spatula to spread over Spiced Streusel. (Pan will be very full, but batter will not overflow during baking.) Tap pan on a kitchen towel-lined counter a few times to settle batter and release any air bubbles.
5. Bake until a wooden pick inserted near center comes out clean, 1 hour and 10 minutes to 1 hour and 15 minutes. Let cool in pan for 30 minutes. Invert cake onto a wire rack, and let cool completely. Pour Citrus Glaze over cooled cake, letting glaze drip down sides. Garnish with Cranberry Powder, if desired.

SPICED STREUSEL
Makes about ⅓ cup

⅓ cup (42 grams) all-purpose flour
⅓ cup (67 grams) granulated sugar
1½ tablespoons (21 grams) firmly packed light brown sugar
1 tablespoon (6 grams) ground cinnamon
1½ teaspoons (3 grams) Chinese five-spice powder
1½ tablespoons (21 grams) unsalted butter, softened

1. In a small bowl, whisk together flour, sugars, cinnamon, and five-spice powder. Using your fingers, cut in butter until mixture has the texture of dry sand.

CITRUS GLAZE
Makes about 1 cup

2¼ cups (270 grams) confectioners' sugar
1 to 3 teaspoons (2 to 6 grams) tightly packed orange zest
1 teaspoon (5 grams) fresh orange juice
1 to 3 tablespoons (15 to 45 grams) whole milk

1. In a small bowl, whisk together confectioners' sugar and orange zest and juice until smooth. Add milk, 1 teaspoon (5 grams) at a time, until desired consistency is reached.

CRANBERRY POWDER
Makes about ¼ cup

½ cup (7 grams) freeze-dried cranberries
1 teaspoon (3 grams) cornstarch

1. In the work bowl of a food processor, place cranberries and cornstarch; pulse until powdered.

APPLE BUTTER BUNDT CAKE

Makes 1 (15-cup) Bundt cake

Loaded with apple butter and a plethora of aromatic spices, this go-to Bundt cake comes together in a flash.

1¾	cups (397 grams) unsalted butter, softened
2½	cups (500 grams) granulated sugar
4	large eggs (200 grams), room temperature
4	cups (500 grams) all-purpose flour
1	tablespoon (15 grams) baking powder
1	teaspoon (2 grams) cinnamon
½	teaspoon (1.5 grams) kosher salt
½	teaspoon (1 gram) ground ginger
½	teaspoon (1 gram) ground nutmeg
2	(9-ounce) jar (255 grams) apple butter*
1	large McIntosh apple (136 grams), grated (about ⅔ cup)

Confectioners' sugar, for dusting

1. Preheat oven to 350°F (180°C).
2. In the bowl of a stand mixer fitted with the paddle attachment, beat butter at medium speed until smooth, about 1 minute. Add granulated sugar, and beat until fluffy, 3 to 4 minutes, stopping to scrape sides of bowl. Add eggs, one at a time, beating well after each addition. (Mixture may look curdled at this point, but batter will come together.)

3. In a medium bowl, whisk together flour, baking powder, cinnamon, salt, ginger, and nutmeg. With mixer on low speed, add flour mixture to butter mixture in two additions alternately with apple butter, beginning and ending with flour mixture, beating just until combined after each addition. Stir in grated apple.
4. Spray a 15-cup Bundt pan with baking spray with flour. Spoon batter into prepared pan.
5. Bake until a wooden pick inserted near center comes out clean, about 1 hour and 15 minutes. Let cool in pan for 15 minutes. Invert cake onto a wire rack, and let cool completely. Dust with confectioners' sugar just before serving.

We used Dickenson's Country Apple Butter.

HUMMINGBIRD BUNDT CAKE

Makes 1 (15-cup) Bundt cake

Think of this Bundt as the frosted layer cake's laid-back cousin. It requires less effort to make but packs all the same spiced, fruity flavor of the original. Bananas and whole milk keep the cake moist and flavorful for days, but the best part is that tangy, spoon-licking Cream Cheese Icing.

3⅓ cups (417 grams) all-purpose flour
1⅓ cups (267 grams) granulated sugar
1 teaspoon (5 grams) baking powder
1 teaspoon (3 grams) kosher salt
1 teaspoon (2 grams) ground cinnamon
¾ teaspoon (3.75 grams) baking soda
¼ teaspoon ground nutmeg
1½ cups (341 grams) mashed ripe banana
1 cup (224 grams) canola oil
½ cup (120 grams) whole milk, room temperature
3 large eggs (150 grams), room temperature
1 teaspoon (4 grams) vanilla extract
1 cup (200 grams) finely chopped fresh pineapple
½ cup (57 grams) chopped pecans
Cream Cheese Icing (recipe follows)
Garnish: chopped toasted pecans

1. Preheat oven to 350°F (180°C).
2. In a large bowl, sift together flour, sugar, baking powder, salt, cinnamon, baking soda, and nutmeg. Make a well in center.
3. In a medium bowl, stir together banana, oil, milk, eggs, and vanilla. Add banana mixture to flour mixture, stirring just until dry ingredients are moistened. Fold in pineapple.
4. Spray a 15-cup Bundt pan with baking spray with flour. Sprinkle pecans in bottom of prepared pan. Pour batter over pecans, smoothing top with an offset spatula.

5. Bake until a wooden pick inserted near center comes out clean, 55 minutes to 1 hour, covering with foil halfway through baking to prevent excess browning. Let cool in pan for 10 minutes. Invert cake onto a wire rack, and let cool completely. Pour Cream Cheese Icing over cooled cake. Top with toasted pecans, if desired.

CREAM CHEESE ICING
Makes about 1½ cups

3 ounces (86 grams) cream cheese, softened
¼ cup (60 grams) whole milk, room temperature
¼ teaspoon (1 gram) vanilla extract
1¾ cups (210 grams) confectioners' sugar

1. In the bowl of a stand mixer fitted with the paddle attachment, beat cream cheese at medium speed until creamy. Add milk and vanilla, beating until combined. Gradually add confectioners' sugar, beating until smooth. Use immediately.

Photo by Stephen DeVries

ORANGE-SOUR CREAM POUND CAKE

Makes 1 (15-cup) Bundt cake

Tangy with sour cream and popping with citrus, this tender cake needs little more than a final dusting of confectioners' sugar.

1½	cups (340 grams) unsalted butter, softened
2½	cups (500 grams) granulated sugar
6	large eggs (300 grams), room temperature
4	teaspoons (4 grams) orange zest
1	teaspoon (4 grams) vanilla extract
½	teaspoon (2 grams) almond extract
3¼	cups (406 grams) cake flour
½	teaspoon (1.5 grams) kosher salt
¼	teaspoon (1.25 grams) baking soda
1	cup (240 grams) sour cream, room temperature

Garnish: confectioners' sugar

1. Preheat oven to 325°F (170°C).
2. In the bowl of a stand mixer fitted with the paddle attachment, beat butter and granulated sugar at medium speed until fluffy, 3 to 4 minutes, stopping to scrape sides of bowl. Add eggs, one at a time, beating well after each addition. Beat in orange zest and extracts. (Mixture may look slightly curdled at this point, but batter will come together.)
3. In a medium bowl, whisk together flour, salt, and baking soda. With mixer on low speed, gradually add flour mixture to butter mixture alternately with sour cream, beginning and ending with flour mixture, beating just until combined after each addition.

4. Spray a 15-cup Bundt pan with baking spray with flour. Spoon batter into prepared pan. Tap pan on a kitchen towel-lined counter a few times to settle batter and release air bubbles.
5. Bake until a wooden pick inserted near center comes out clean, about 1 hour and 25 minutes, loosely covering with foil to prevent excess browning, if necessary. Let cool in pan for 10 minutes. Invert cake onto a wire rack, and let cool completely. Garnish with confectioners' sugar, if desired.

CANDIED APPLE & PEAR BUNDT CAKE

Makes 1 (15-cup) Bundt cake

With candied apples and pears mixed into the batter, this Bundt cake is the epitome of comforting autumn flavor.

3 cups (600 grams) granulated sugar, divided
½ cup (170 grams) cane syrup
1½ cups (340 grams) plus 2 tablespoons (28 grams) unsalted butter, softened and divided
2 large Granny Smith apples (412 grams), peeled, cored, and sliced
2 Bosc pears (358 grams), peeled, cored, and sliced
5 large eggs (250 grams), room temperature
2 teaspoons (8 grams) vanilla extract
3¼ cups (406 grams) all-purpose flour
2 teaspoons (2 grams) ground cinnamon
1½ teaspoons (4.5 grams) kosher salt
1 teaspoon grated fresh nutmeg
½ teaspoon (2.5 grams) baking soda
1 cup (240 grams) sour cream, room temperature
Cane Syrup Glaze (recipe follows)

1. Preheat oven to 325°F (170°C).

2. In a large skillet, bring 1 cup (200 grams) sugar and cane syrup to a boil over medium-high heat; cook, stirring constantly, until sugar dissolves, about 2 minutes. Stir in 2 tablespoons (28 grams) butter until melted. Add apple and pear; reduce heat to medium, and cook, stirring occasionally, until fruit softens, about 12 minutes. Remove from heat, and let cool completely.

3. In the bowl of a stand mixer fitted with the paddle attachment, beat remaining 1½ cups (340 grams) butter and remaining 2 cups (400 grams) sugar at medium speed until fluffy, 3 to 4 minutes, stopping to scrape sides of bowl. Add eggs, one at a time, beating well after each addition. Beat in vanilla.

4. In a medium bowl, whisk together flour, cinnamon, salt, nutmeg, and baking soda. With mixer on low speed, gradually add flour mixture to butter mixture alternately with sour cream, beginning and ending with flour mixture, beating just until combined after each addition.

5. Reserve 2 tablespoons (36 grams) syrup from fruit mixture for Cane Syrup Glaze. Gently fold fruit mixture and remaining syrup into batter.

6. Spray a 15-cup Bundt pan with baking spray with flour. Spoon batter into prepared pan. Tap pan on a kitchen towel-lined counter a few times to settle batter and release any air bubbles.

7. Bake until a wooden pick inserted near center comes out clean, 1 hour to 1 hour and 10 minutes. Let cool in pan for 10 minutes. Loosen cake from center of pan using a small offset spatula. Invert cake onto a wire rack placed over a parchment paper-lined rimmed baking sheet, and let cool completely. Drizzle Cane Syrup Glaze onto cooled cake.

CANE SYRUP GLAZE

Makes about ¾ cup

2 cups (240 grams) confectioners' sugar
2 tablespoons (30 grams) whole buttermilk
2 tablespoons (36 grams) fruit-cane syrup, reserved from Candied Apple & Pear Bundt Cake (recipe precedes)

1. In a small bowl, whisk together all ingredients until combined. Use immediately.

PRO TIP
If your local grocery stores don't carry cane syrup, consider substituting with Lyle's Golden Syrup, a popular British brand often sold in the international aisle in stores.

LEMON-BLUEBERRY BUTTERMILK POUND CAKE

Makes 1 (15-cup) Bundt cake

This tender Bundt cake offers the flavor trifecta: tangy, tart, and sweet.

1½	cups (340 grams) unsalted butter, softened
3	cups (600 grams) granulated sugar
6	large eggs (300 grams), room temperature
1	teaspoon (4 grams) vanilla extract
½	teaspoon (2 grams) almond extract
3½	cups (438 grams) all-purpose flour
1	teaspoon (3 grams) kosher salt
½	teaspoon (2.5 grams) baking powder
1	cup (240 grams) whole buttermilk, room temperature
1	tablespoon (3 grams) lemon zest
1	tablespoon (15 grams) fresh lemon juice
1½	cups (222 grams) fresh blueberries

Buttermilk Glaze (recipe follows)

1. Preheat oven to 325°F (170°C).
2. In the bowl of a stand mixer fitted with the paddle attachment, beat butter and sugar at medium speed until fluffy, 6 to 7 minutes, stopping to scrape sides of bowl. Add eggs, one at a time, beating well after each addition, stopping to scrape sides of bowl. Beat in extracts.
3. In a large bowl, whisk together flour, salt, and baking powder. In a small bowl, combine buttermilk, and lemon zest and juice. With mixer on low speed, add flour mixture to butter mixture in three additions alternately with buttermilk mixture, beginning and ending with flour mixture, beating just until combined after each addition.

4. Spray a 15-cup Bundt pan with baking spray with flour. Spoon two-thirds of batter into prepared pan. Tap pan on a kitchen towel-lined counter a few times to settle batter and release any air bubbles. Sprinkle blueberries onto batter in pan, and gently press into batter, being careful not to let berries touch sides of pan. Spoon remaining batter on top of blueberries, smoothing top with an offset spatula. Tap pan on kitchen towel-lined counter serveral times to release air bubbles.
5. Bake until a wooden pick inserted near center comes out clean, about 1 hour and 20 minutes. Let cool in pan for 15 minutes. Invert cake onto a wire rack, and let cool completely. Drizzle Buttermilk Glaze onto cooled cake.

BUTTERMILK GLAZE

Makes ⅔ cup

1½	cups (180 grams) confectioners' sugar
3	tablespoons (45 grams) whole buttermilk

1. In a medium bowl, whisk together confectioners' sugar and buttermilk until smooth. Use immediately.

BUTTER CAKE WITH BROWNED BUTTER STRAWBERRY SYRUP

Makes 1 (15-cup) Bundt cake

Simple pound cake gets a decadent drizzle of warmly spiced browned butter and strawberry syrup.

3 cups (681 grams) unsalted butter, softened and divided
3½ cups (700 grams) granulated sugar, divided
4 large eggs (200 grams), room temperature
1 teaspoon (4 grams) vanilla extract
4 cups (500 grams) all-purpose flour
1¾ teaspoons (5.25 grams) kosher salt
1 teaspoon (5 grams) baking powder
1⅓ cups (320 grams) whole milk, room temperature
4 cups (600 grams) quartered fresh strawberries
¼ teaspoon ground cardamom
¼ cup (85 grams) light corn syrup

1. Preheat oven to 325°F (170°C).
2. In the bowl of a stand mixer fitted with the paddle attachment, beat 2 cups butter (454 grams) and 3 cups (600 grams) sugar at medium speed until fluffy, 3 to 4 minutes, stopping to scrape sides of bowl. Add eggs, one at a time, beating well after each addition. Beat in vanilla.
3. In a large bowl, sift together flour, salt, and baking powder. With mixer on low speed, gradually add flour mixture to butter mixture alternately with milk, beginning and ending with flour mixture, beating just until combined after each addition.
4. Spray a 15-cup Bundt pan with baking spray with flour. Spoon batter into prepared pan.
5. Bake until a wooden pick inserted near center comes out clean, about 1½ hours. Let cool in pan for 10 minutes. Invert onto a wire rack, and let cool completely.

6. In a small bowl, stir together strawberries, cardamom, and remaining ½ cup (100 grams) sugar. Let stand at room temperature until strawberries have softened, about 1 hour. Drain strawberries, reserving ½ cup strawberry juice.
7. In a medium saucepan, melt remaining 1 cup (227 grams) butter over medium heat. Cook, stirring frequently, until butter turns a medium-brown color and has a nutty aroma, about 10 minutes. Remove from heat; whisk in corn syrup and reserved ½ cup strawberry juice. Serve syrup and strawberries with cake.

PRO TIP
You will make quite a bit of browned butter strawberry syrup and may have some left over. Use this leftover syrup on ice cream, French toast, waffles, or pancakes.

LEMON POPPY SEED BUNDT CAKE

Makes 1 (10-cup) Bundt cake

Poppy seeds give this refreshingly tangy cake a slight crunch.

1¼ cups (284 grams) unsalted butter, softened
2½ cups (500 grams) granulated sugar, divided
5 large eggs (250 grams), room temperature
2 tablespoons (14 grams) tightly packed lemon zest
⅓ cup (80 grams) plus 2 teaspoons (10 grams) fresh lemon juice, divided
1½ teaspoons (6 grams) vanilla extract
2½ cups (313 grams) unbleached cake flour
1½ tablespoons (13.5 grams) poppy seeds
1¼ teaspoons (3.75 grams) kosher salt
½ teaspoon (2.5 grams) baking soda
1 cup (240 grams) sour cream, room temperature
Lemon Glaze (recipe follows)

1. Preheat oven to 325°F (170°C).

2. In the bowl of a stand mixer fitted with the paddle attachment, beat butter and 2¼ cups (450 grams) sugar at medium speed until fluffy, 3 to 4 minutes, stopping to scrape sides of bowl. Add eggs, one at a time, beating until well combined after each addition and stopping to scrape sides of bowl. Beat in lemon zest, 2 teaspoons (10 grams) lemon juice, and vanilla. (Mixture may look slightly curdled at this point, but batter will come together.)

3. In a medium bowl, whisk together flour, poppy seeds, salt, and baking soda. Add flour mixture to butter mixture alternately with sour cream, beginning and ending with flour mixture, beating just until combined after each addition and stopping to scrape sides of bowl.

4. Spray a 10-cup Bundt pan with baking spray with flour. Spoon batter into prepared pan. Tap pan on a kitchen towel-lined counter a few times to settle batter and release any air bubbles. (Pan will be quite full, but batter will not overflow during baking.)

5. Bake until a wooden pick inserted near center comes out clean, 1 hour to 1 hour and 5 minutes, rotating pan halfway through baking and loosely covering with foil to prevent excess browning, if necessary. Let cool in pan for 20 minutes.

6. In a small bowl, stir together remaining ⅓ cup lemon juice (80 grams) and remaining ¼ cup (50 grams) sugar.

7. Loosen cake from center of pan using a small offset spatula. Invert cake onto a wire rack placed over a rimmed baking sheet. Gently brush cake all over with lemon juice mixture, and let cool completely.

8. Spoon and spread Lemon Glaze over top of cooled cake before serving.

LEMON GLAZE
Makes ½ cup

1½ cups (180 grams) confectioners' sugar, sifted
2 tablespoons (30 grams) fresh lemon juice

1. In a small bowl, stir together confectioners' sugar and lemon juice until smooth and well combined. Use immediately.

Photo by Alison Miksch

SATSUMA-VANILLA BUNDT CAKE

Makes 1 (6-cup) Bundt cake

With satsuma zest mixed into the batter and a sweet Satsuma Glaze, this Bundt has a double dose of bright citrus flavor.

¾   cup (170 grams) unsalted butter, softened
1½ cups (300 grams) granulated sugar
3   large eggs (150 grams), room temperature
1   large egg yolk (19 grams), room temperature
1   tablespoon (18 grams) vanilla bean paste
1   tablespoon (3 grams) satsuma zest (about 2 satsumas)
1½ cups (188 grams) all-purpose flour
¾   teaspoon (2.25 grams) kosher salt
½   cup (120 grams) sour cream, room temperature
Satsuma Glaze (recipe follows)
Garnish: satsuma zest

1. Preheat oven to 350°F (180°C).
2. In the bowl of a stand mixer fitted with a paddle attachment, beat butter and sugar at medium speed until light and fluffy, 3 to 4 minutes, stopping to scrape sides of bowl. Add eggs and egg yolk, one at a time, beating well after each addition. Stir in vanilla bean paste and satsuma zest. (Mixture may look slightly curdled at this point, but batter will come together.)
3. In a medium bowl, whisk together flour and salt. With mixer on low speed, gradually add flour mixture to butter mixture alternately with sour cream, beginning and ending with flour mixture, beating just until combined after each addition.
4. Generously spray a 6-cup Bundt pan with baking spray with flour. Spoon batter into prepared pan. Tap pan on a kitchen towel-lined counter a few times to settle batter and release any air bubbles.

5. Bake until a wooden pick inserted near center comes out clean, 40 to 45 minutes. Let cool in pan for 10 minutes. Using a small offset spatula, loosen cake from center of pan. Invert cake onto a wire rack placed over a parchment paper-lined rimmed baking sheet, and let cool completely. Pour Satsuma Glaze over cooled cake. Garnish with satsuma zest, if desired.

SATSUMA GLAZE
Makes about ¾ cup

2¼ cups (270 grams) confectioners' sugar
4 to 5 tablespoons (60 to 75 grams) fresh satsuma juice

1. In a small bowl, whisk together confectioners' sugar and 4 tablespoons (60 grams) satsuma juice until smooth. Thin with remaining 1 tablespoon (15 grams) satsuma juice, 1 teaspoon (5 grams) at a time, if necessary. Use immediately.

PRO TIP
If you have trouble locating satsumas or they are currently not in season, try substituting with clementines, tangerines, or navel oranges, using the same amount of zest and juice.

SWIRLED & TWIRLED

HIDING SURPRISE SWIRLS OF CREAM CHEESE, PECANS, JELLY, AND MORE, EACH OF THESE SWEETLY SWIRLED BUNDT CAKES SHOWS THERE'S PLENTY OF EXCITEMENT LYING BENEATH THE SURFACE

PEACH POUND CAKE

Makes 1 (15-cup) Bundt cake

A rich, tangy dose of buttermilk and swirls of cream cheese complement the bright sweetness of the peaches in this decadent pound cake.

1½ cups (340 grams) unsalted butter, softened
2⅓ cups (467 grams) granulated sugar, divided
5   large eggs (250 grams), room temperature
½   teaspoon (2 grams) almond extract
2¾ cups (344 grams) plus 2 tablespoons (16 grams)
    all-purpose flour, divided
¼   cup (30 grams) coconut flour
1   teaspoon (3 grams) kosher salt
½   cup (120 grams) plus 2 tablespoons (30 grams)
    whole buttermilk, room temperature and divided
2   cups (400 grams) diced and peeled fresh peaches
    (about 3 medium peaches)
½   cup (112 grams) cream cheese, softened
Buttermilk Glaze (recipe follows)

1. Preheat oven to 325°F (170°C).
2. In the bowl of a stand mixer fitted with the paddle attachment, beat butter and 2 cups (400 grams) sugar at medium speed until fluffy, 6 to 8 minutes, stopping to scrape sides of bowl. Add eggs, one at a time, beating well after each addition. Beat in almond extract.
3. In a medium bowl, whisk together 2¾ cups (344 grams) all-purpose flour, coconut flour, and salt. With mixer on low speed, gradually add flour mixture to butter mixture alternately with ½ cup (120 grams) buttermilk, beginning and ending with flour mixture, beating just until combined after each addition. Fold in peaches. Transfer batter to a large bowl; set aside.

4. Clean bowl of stand mixer and paddle attachment. Using the paddle attachment, beat cream cheese, remaining ⅓ cup (67 grams) sugar, and remaining 2 tablespoons (16 grams) all-purpose flour at medium speed until creamy, 3 to 4 minutes, stopping to scrape sides of bowl. Beat in remaining 2 tablespoons (30 grams) buttermilk until well combined.
5. Spray a 15-cup Bundt pan with baking spray with flour. Spoon half of batter into prepared pan; make a well in center, leaving a ¼-inch border around edges of pan, and spoon cream cheese mixture into well. Spoon remaining batter over cream cheese mixture. Using a knife, gently swirl batter and cream cheese mixture.
6. Bake until a wooden pick inserted near center comes out clean, 1½ hours to 1 hour and 35 minutes, covering with foil after 1 hour of baking to prevent excess browning. Let cool in pan for 20 minutes. Invert cake onto a wire rack, and let cool completely. Spoon Buttermilk Glaze onto cooled cake.

BUTTERMILK GLAZE
Makes about ½ cup

½   cup (112 grams) cream cheese, softened
1½ tablespoons (21 grams) unsalted butter, softened
½   cup (60 grams) confectioners' sugar
¼   cup plus 2 tablespoons (90 grams) whole buttermilk

1. In the bowl of a stand mixer fitted with the paddle attachment, beat cream cheese and butter at medium speed until creamy, 3 to 4 minutes. Reduce mixer speed to low, and gradually add confectioners' sugar, beating until combined. Add buttermilk, beating until smooth. Use immediately.

IN-FLIGHT BUNDT CAKE

Makes 1 (10-cup) Bundt cake

Inspired by my former days as a flight attendant, this Bundt is for all my fellow travel enthusiasts. I married the familiar flavor combo of coffee and spiced cookies served on flights into one crave-worthy cookie butter-packed cake with the creamiest, dreamiest cream cheese swirl.

8	ounces (226 grams) cream cheese, softened
1¾	cups (350 grams) plus 3 tablespoons (36 grams) granulated sugar, divided
2⅓	cups (292 grams) plus 1 tablespoon (8 grams) all-purpose flour, divided
1½	teaspoons (3.75 grams) kosher salt, divided
5	large eggs (250 grams), room temperature and divided
¼	cup (24 grams) espresso powder
1	tablespoon (15 grams) water
⅔	cup (160 grams) whole milk, room temperature
2	teaspoons (8 grams) vanilla extract
1	cup (227 grams) unsalted butter, softened
½	cup (128 grams) creamy cookie butter*
¾	teaspoon (3.75 grams) baking powder

Cookie Butter Glaze (recipe follows)
Garnish: roughly crushed speculoos cookies*

1. Preheat oven to 325°F (170°C).
2. In the bowl of a stand mixer fitted with the paddle attachment, beat cream cheese, 3 tablespoons (36 grams) sugar, 1 tablespoon (8 grams) flour, and ¼ teaspoon salt at medium speed until smooth and creamy, 1 to 2 minutes, stopping to scrape sides of bowl. Add 1 egg (50 grams); beat until smooth and well combined, about 2 minutes, stopping to scrape sides of bowl. Transfer to a small bowl; cover and refrigerate until ready to use.
3. In a small bowl, stir together espresso powder and 1 tablespoon (15 grams) water until well combined. Stir in milk and vanilla.
4. Clean bowl of stand mixer and paddle attachment. Using the paddle attachment, beat butter, cookie butter, and remaining 1¾ cups (350 grams) sugar at medium-low speed just until combined. Increase mixer speed to medium, and beat until fluffy, about 3 minutes, stopping to scrape sides of bowl. Add remaining 4 eggs (200 grams), one at a time, beating well after each addition.
5. In a medium bowl, whisk together baking powder, remaining 2⅓ cups (292 grams) flour, and remaining 1¼ teaspoons (3.75 grams) salt. With mixer on low speed, add flour mixture to butter mixture alternately with milk mixture, beginning and ending with flour mixture, beating until combined after each addition and stopping to scrape sides of bowl.

6. Spray a 10-cup Bundt pan with baking spray with flour. Spoon half of batter (about 678 grams) into prepared pan. Tap pan on a kitchen towel-lined counter a few times to settle batter and release any air bubbles. Spoon dollops of chilled cream cheese mixture onto batter in pan alternately with small dollops of batter; layer and repeat as needed until cream cheese mixture is finished. Drag a butter knife back and forth through batter and cream cheese mixture to swirl. (It's OK if cream cheese mixture touches sides of pan.) Spoon and spread remaining batter on top; gently tap pan on counter a few times to evenly spread batter and release any air bubbles. (Pan will be quite full, but batter will not overflow during baking.)
7. Bake until a wooden pick inserted near center comes out clean, 58 minutes to 1 hour, rotating pan halfway through baking and loosely covering with foil to prevent excess browning, if necessary. (It's OK if some cream cheese mixture peeks through top.) Let cool in pan for 35 minutes. Invert cake onto a wire rack placed over a parchment paper-lined rimmed baking sheet, and let cool completely.
8. Place Cookie Butter Glaze in a squeezable plastic icing bottle fitted with a ¼-inch round tip (Wilton No. 12). Carefully spoon glaze onto cake. Transfer to a serving plate. Garnish with cookies, if desired.

*We used Lotus Biscoff Creamy Cookie Butter and Lotus Biscoff Cookies.

COOKIE BUTTER GLAZE
Makes about ⅔ cup

½	cup (60 grams) confectioners' sugar
½	cup (128 grams) creamy cookie butter
3	tablespoons (45 grams) whole milk, room temperature
½	teaspoon (2 grams) vanilla extract
¼	teaspoon kosher salt

1. In a small bowl, whisk together all ingredients until smooth and well combined. Use immediately.

CINNAMON SWIRL BUNDT CAKE

Makes 1 (15-cup) Bundt cake

Win brunch any day of the year with this sweet, cinnamon-swirled Bundt cake topped with luscious Cream Cheese Glaze.

1½ cups (340 grams) unsalted butter, softened
2¾ cups (550 grams) plus ⅓ cup (67 grams) granulated sugar, divided
7 large eggs (350 grams), room temperature
2½ teaspoons (10 grams) vanilla extract, divided
3½ cups (438 grams) plus 2 tablespoons (16 grams) all-purpose flour, divided
1 teaspoon (3 grams) kosher salt
1 cup (240 grams) plus 2 tablespoons (30 grams) sour cream, room temperature and divided
4 ounces (113 grams) cream cheese, softened
1½ teaspoons (3 grams) ground cinnamon
⅛ teaspoon ground nutmeg
Cream Cheese Glaze (recipe follows)
Garnish: ground cinnamon

1. Preheat oven to 325°F (170°C).
2. In the bowl of a stand mixer fitted with the paddle attachment, beat butter and 2¾ cups (550 grams) sugar at medium speed until fluffy, 6 to 7 minutes, stopping to scrape sides of bowl. Add eggs, one at a time, beating well after each addition. Stir in 1½ teaspoons (6 grams) vanilla.
3. In a medium bowl, sift together 3½ cups (438 grams) flour and salt. With mixer on low speed, gradually add flour mixture to butter mixture alternately with 1 cup (240 grams) sour cream, beginning and ending with flour mixture, beating just until combined after each addition.
4. In a medium bowl, beat cream cheese, remaining ⅓ cup (67 grams) sugar, remaining 2 tablespoons (30 grams) sour cream, and remaining 1 teaspoon (4 grams) vanilla with a mixer at medium speed until smooth. Add cinnamon, nutmeg, and remaining 2 tablespoons (16 grams) flour, and beat until smooth.
5. Spray a 15-cup Bundt pan with baking spray with flour. Spoon half of batter into prepared pan. Tap pan on a kitchen towel-lined counter a few times to settle batter and release any air bubbles. Add cream cheese mixture, leaving a ¼-inch border around edges of pan; top with remaining batter. Using a knife, gently swirl batter and cream cheese mixture, making sure cream cheese mixture does not touch sides of pan. Tap pan on kitchen towel-lined counter a few times to settle batter and release any air bubbles.
6. Bake for 1 hour, rotating pan halfway through baking. Cover with foil, and bake until an instant-read thermometer inserted near center registers 200°F (93°C) to 210°F (99°C), 15 to 20 minutes more. Let cool in pan for 30 minutes. Invert cake onto a wire rack, and let cool completely. Spoon Cream Cheese Glaze onto cooled cake. Garnish with cinnamon, if desired.

CREAM CHEESE GLAZE

Makes 1¼ cups

6 ounces (170 grams) cream cheese, softened
⅓ cup (40 grams) confectioners' sugar
1½ tablespoons (22.5 grams) whole milk, room temperature

1. In a small bowl, whisk together all ingredients until smooth. Use immediately.

STRAWBERRY SWIRL POUND CAKE

Makes 1 (15-cup) Bundt cake

Strawberry swirls forever. This glammed up simple pound cake with a brilliant strawberry swirl and sweet citrus glaze.

1   cup (227 grams) unsalted butter, softened
8   ounces (226 grams) cream cheese, softened
3   cups (600 grams) granulated sugar
4   large eggs (200 grams), room temperature
1½ teaspoons (6 grams) vanilla extract
4   cups (500 grams) all-purpose flour
1   tablespoon (15 grams) baking powder
½   teaspoon (1.5 grams) kosher salt
¾   cup (180 grams) whole buttermilk, room temperature
1   (8.2-ounce) jar (232 grams) strawberry fruit spread*
2   tablespoons (16 grams) cornstarch
Buttermilk Orange Glaze (recipe follows)

1. Preheat oven to 325°F (170°C).
2. In the bowl of a stand mixer fitted with the paddle attachment, beat butter, cream cheese, and sugar at medium speed until fluffy, 4 to 5 minutes, stopping to scrape sides of bowl. Add eggs, one at a time, beating just until combined after each addition. Beat in vanilla.
3. In a large bowl, whisk together flour, baking powder, and salt. With mixer on low speed, gradually add flour mixture to butter mixture alternately with buttermilk, beginning and ending with flour mixture, beating just until combined after each addition.
4. In a small bowl, stir together fruit spread and cornstarch.
5. Spray a 15-cup Bundt pan with baking spray with flour. Spoon 5 cups (about 1,157 grams) batter into prepared pan. Dollop fruit spread mixture onto batter in pan, and swirl together with a wooden skewer. Spoon remaining batter (about 700 grams) onto fruit spread mixture, and swirl with wooden skewer.

6. Bake until a wooden pick inserted near center comes out clean, about 1½ hours. Let cool in pan on a wire rack for 15 minutes. Invert cake onto wire rack, and let cool completely. Spoon Buttermilk Orange Glaze onto cooled cake.

We used Bonne Maman Intense Strawberry Fruit Spread.

BUTTERMILK ORANGE GLAZE

Makes ⅔ cup

1½ cups (180 grams) confectioners' sugar
2   tablespoons (30 grams) whole milk
1   tablespoon (15 grams) orange liqueur

1. In a small bowl, whisk together all ingredients until smooth. Use immediately.

BANANA BUNDT CAKE WITH CREAM CHEESE SWIRL

Makes 1 (10-cup) Bundt cake

Easy to make and impressive to serve, this banana cake is filled with warm spices and cream cheese ribbons.

1¼ cups (300 grams) mashed ripe banana (about 3 medium bananas)
1½ cups (360 grams) whole buttermilk, room temperature
¾ cup (165 grams) firmly packed light brown sugar
½ cup (113 grams) plus 2 tablespoons (28 grams) unsalted butter, melted and divided
¼ cup (50 grams) plus 3 tablespoons (36 grams) granulated sugar, divided
¼ cup (56 grams) vegetable oil
4 large eggs (200 grams), room temperature and divided
1 tablespoon (15 grams) bourbon
1½ teaspoons (9 grams) vanilla bean paste, divided
3 cups (375 grams) plus 2 teaspoons (6 grams) all-purpose flour, divided
2 teaspoons (10 grams) baking powder
1 teaspoon (5 grams) baking soda
1 teaspoon (3 grams) kosher salt
1 teaspoon (2 grams) ground cinnamon
¼ teaspoon ground nutmeg
6 ounces (170 grams) cream cheese, softened
¼ cup (50 grams) sanding sugar

1. Preheat oven to 350°F (180°C).
2. In the bowl of a stand mixer fitted with the paddle attachment, combine banana, buttermilk, brown sugar, ½ cup (113 grams) melted butter, ¼ cup (50 grams) granulated sugar, oil, 3 eggs (150 grams), bourbon, and 1 teaspoon (6 grams) vanilla bean paste; beat at medium-low speed until well combined, about 2 minutes, stopping to scrape sides of bowl.
3. In a large bowl, whisk together 3 cups (375 grams) flour, baking powder, baking soda, salt, cinnamon, and nutmeg. With mixer on low speed, gradually add flour mixture to banana mixture, beating until combined and stopping to scrape sides of bowl. Transfer batter to a large bowl.
4. Clean bowl of stand mixer and paddle attachment. Using the paddle attachment, beat cream cheese, remaining 3 tablespoons (36 grams) granulated sugar, and remaining 2 teaspoons (6 grams) flour at medium speed until smooth and well combined, 1 to 2 minutes, stopping to scrape sides of bowl. Add remaining 1 egg (50 grams) and remaining ½ teaspoon (3 grams) vanilla bean paste; beat at medium speed until smooth and well combined, about 2 minutes, stopping to scrape sides of bowl.
5. Spray a 10-cup Bundt pan with baking spray with flour. Spoon 4 cups batter (about 956 grams) into prepared pan; forcefully tap pan on counter several times to release as many air bubbles as possible. Spoon a ring of cream cheese mixture in center of batter in pan, leaving a ¼-inch border around inside and outer edges of pan. (Cream cheese mixture will have the consistency of cheesecake filling, so you will be able to almost drizzle, rather than dollop, the mixture; it is fine if cream cheese mixture touches sides of pan in places.) Using a butter knife, gently swirl cream cheese mixture into batter using a folding motion. Spoon remaining batter on top, covering cream cheese mixture. Do not tap pan. (Pan will be quite full, but batter will not overflow during baking.)
6. Bake for 45 minutes. Cover with foil, and bake until a wooden pick inserted near center comes out clean and an instant-read thermometer registers at least 200°F (93°C), 15 to 20 minutes more. (It's OK if some cream cheese mixture peeks through surface of cake.) Let cool in pan for 20 minutes. Invert cake onto a wire rack placed over a parchment-lined rimmed baking sheet, and let cool completely.
7. Brush cooled cake with remaining 2 tablespoons (28 grams) melted butter; cover with sanding sugar, pressing gently to help adhere. Serve immediately.

FREEZE NOW, BAKE LATER
Bananas are excellent produce to stock in the freezer. Keep the bananas in their peel (this protects them from freezer burn and odors), and store in a resealable plastic freezer bag. Once you're ready to bake, allow the bananas to defrost before peeling. The bananas should come out as purée—freezing breaks down the cell walls and naturally produces a mash.

PEANUT BUTTER AND JELLY SWIRL BUNDT CAKE

Makes 1 (10-cup) Bundt cake

Your favorite childhood sandwich has been upgraded to an out-of-this-world frosted Bundt cake with a gorgeous fruity swirl that is perfect for any time of day all year long.

1¼	cups (284 grams) unsalted butter, softened and divided	
1	cup (200 grams) granulated sugar	
1	cup (220 grams) firmly packed dark brown sugar	
½	cup (128 grams) plus 2 tablespoons (32 grams) creamy peanut butter, divided	
4	large eggs (250 grams), room temperature	
2	teaspoons (18 grams) vanilla extract	
3	cups (375 grams) all-purpose flour	
1	teaspoon (5 grams) baking powder	
½	teaspoon (2 grams) kosher salt	
1	cup (240 grams) plus 2 tablespoons (30 grams) whole milk, room temperature and divided	
1	(8.2-ounce) jar (235 grams) strawberry fruit spread*	
2	tablespoons (16 grams) cornstarch	
2	cups (240 grams) confectioners' sugar	

1. Preheat oven to 325°F (170°C).

2. In the bowl of a stand mixer fitted with the paddle attachment, beat 1 cup (227 grams) butter, granulated sugar, brown sugar, and ½ cup (128 grams) peanut butter at medium speed until light and fluffy, 3 to 4 minutes, stopping to scrape sides of bowl. Add eggs, one at a time, beating well after each addition. Beat in vanilla.

3. In a medium bowl, whisk together flour, baking powder, and salt. With mixer on low speed, gradually add flour mixture to butter mixture alternately with 1 cup (240 grams) milk, beginning and ending with flour mixture, beating just until combined after each addition.

4. In a small bowl, stir together fruit spread and cornstarch until well combined.

5. Spray a 10-cup Bundt pan with baking spray with flour. Spoon 4 cups (about 1,024 grams) batter into prepared pan; make a well in center, leaving a ¼-inch border around edges of pan, and spoon fruit spread mixture into well. Gently spoon remaining batter onto fruit spread mixture, and smooth top with a small offset spatula. Place a knife halfway into batter, and swirl.

6. Bake for 45 minutes. Cover with foil, and bake until a wooden pick inserted near center comes out clean, 20 to 30 minutes more. Let cool in pan for 10 minutes. Invert cake onto a wire rack, and let cool completely.

7. In a large bowl, whisk together confectioners' sugar, remaining ¼ cup (57 grams) butter, remaining 2 tablespoons (32 grams) peanut butter, and remaining 2 tablespoons (30 grams) milk until combined and smooth. Spread on top of cooled cake.

We used Bonne Maman Intense Strawberry Fruit Spread.

PRO TIP

We opted for fruit spread rather than a jam or jelly. Why? Fruit spread is made with no sugar added, meaning it packs the most intense fruit flavor of any product available. Its thicker consistency also holds up well when baked.

PEPPERMINT SWIRL POUND CAKE

Makes 1 (10-cup) Bundt cake

Classic pound cake goes from simple to showstopping thanks to a double dose of peppermint candies and peppermint extract swirled into marbled vanilla and cocoa batters. Topped with Cream Cheese Glaze, this cake strikes the perfect balance between sweet and tangy.

1½	cups (340 grams) unsalted butter, softened
8	ounces (226 grams) cream cheese, softened
2	cups (400 grams) granulated sugar
1	cup (220 grams) firmly packed light brown sugar
6	large eggs (300 grams), room temperature
2	teaspoons (8 grams) vanilla extract
3	cups (375 grams) all-purpose flour
1	teaspoon (3 grams) kosher salt
1	teaspoon (5 grams) baking powder
¼	cup (60 grams) whole milk, room temperature
½	cup (42 grams) Dutch process cocoa powder, sifted
1	teaspoon (4 grams) peppermint extract

Cream Cheese Glaze (recipe follows)
Garnish: roughly crushed round peppermint candies
　　　　 (about 6 candies)

1. Preheat oven to 325°F (150°C).
2. In the bowl of a stand mixer fitted with the paddle attachment, beat butter and cream cheese at medium speed until smooth, about 1 minute. Add sugars; beat until fluffy, 3 to 4 minutes, stopping to scrape sides of bowl. Add eggs, one at a time, beating well after each addition. Beat in vanilla. (Mixture may look curdled at this point, but batter will come together.)
3. In a medium bowl, whisk together flour, salt, and baking powder. With mixer on low speed, add flour mixture to butter mixture in two additions alternately with milk, beginning and ending with flour mixture, beating just until combined. Spoon 2 cups (about 406 grams) batter into a medium bowl. Add cocoa and peppermint extract to remaining batter in stand mixer bowl; stir until combined.

4. Spray a 10-cup Bundt pan with baking spray with flour. Using a 1-tablespoon spring-loaded scoop, alternately scoop batters into prepared pan; using the tip of a knife, gently swirl batters together. Tap pan on a kitchen towel-lined counter a few times to settle batter and release any air bubbles.
5. Bake until a wooden pick inserted near center comes out clean, about 1 hour and 10 minutes to 1 hour and 15 minutes, covering with foil after 45 minutes of baking to prevent excess browning. Let cool in pan for 10 minutes. Run a knife around edges of pan. Invert cake onto a wire rack, and let cool completely.
6. Spoon Cream Cheese Glaze onto cooled cake. Garnish with peppermint candies, if desired.

CREAM CHEESE GLAZE

Makes ⅔ cup

1	cup (120 grams) confectioners' sugar
¼	cup (56 grams) cream cheese, softened
½	teaspoon (1 gram) kosher salt
¼	cup (60 grams) heavy whipping cream

1. In a small bowl, stir together confectioners' sugar, cream cheese, and salt until well combined. Stir in cream until smooth. Use immediately.

POUND CAKE PERFECTION

A CLASSIC FOR A REASON,
POUND CAKE IS THE PERFECT
PLATFORM FOR A NUMBER
OF FLAVOR PAIRINGS, FROM
CREAMY TRES LECHES TO
NUTTY ITALIAN CREAM TO
REFRESHING PEPPERMINT

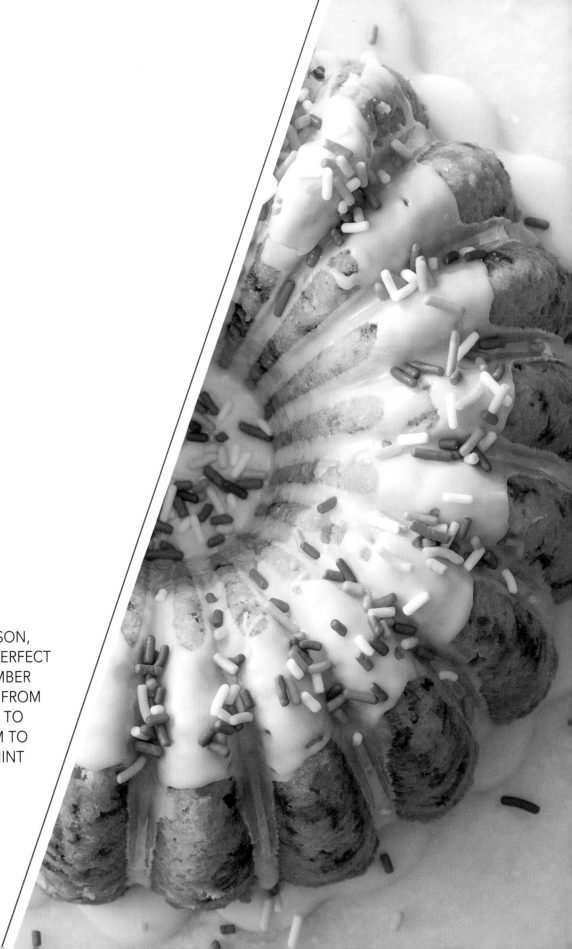

BROWN SUGAR BUNDT CAKE WITH TOASTED SESAME FROSTING

Makes 1 (10-cup) Bundt cake

This golden brown sugar pound cake receives a modern twist with a creamy tahini frosting crown and a sprinkling of toasted sesame seeds.

¾   cup (170 grams) unsalted butter, softened
1½ cups (330 grams) firmly packed light brown sugar
3   large eggs (150 grams), room temperature
3   cups (375 grams) all-purpose flour
1½ teaspoons (7.5 grams) baking powder
¾   teaspoon (3.75 grams) baking soda
¾   teaspoon (2.25 grams) kosher salt
½   teaspoon (1 gram) ground cinnamon
1¼ cups (300 grams) whole buttermilk, room temperature
1   teaspoon (4 grams) vanilla extract
Toasted Sesame Frosting (recipe follows)
Garnish: toasted sesame seeds

1. Preheat oven to 300°F (150°C).
2. In the bowl of a stand mixer fitted with the paddle attachment, beat butter and brown sugar at medium speed until fluffy, 3 to 4 minutes, stopping to scrape sides of bowl. Add eggs, one at a time, beating well after each addition. Add flour, baking powder, baking soda, salt, and cinnamon, beating just until combined. Beat in buttermilk and vanilla just until combined.
3. Spray a 10-cup Bundt pan with baking spray with flour. Spoon batter into prepared pan, smoothing top with an offset spatula.

4. Bake until a wooden pick inserted near center comes out clean, about 1 hour and 5 minutes. (Cake will rise considerably but will not overflow pan.) Let cool in pan for 10 minutes. Invert cake onto a wire rack, and let cool completely. Spread Toasted Sesame Frosting onto cooled cake. Garnish with sesame seeds, if desired.

TOASTED SESAME FROSTING
Makes about 1 cup

⅓   cup (75 grams) tahini
¼   cup (57 grams) unsalted butter, room temperature (see Note)
½   cup (60 grams) confectioners' sugar
¼   teaspoon kosher salt

1. In a small bowl, stir together tahini and butter until smooth. Add confectioners' sugar and salt, stirring until smooth. Use immediately.

Note: *For this frosting to come together properly, it is especially important that your butter is room temperature.*

CLASSIC VANILLA POUND CAKE

Makes 1 (10-cup) Bundt cake

You can choose your flavor with this incredibly simple, perfectly sweet pound cake. Go almond, lemon, or vanilla. (See Flavor Variations.)

1½   cups (340 grams) unsalted butter, softened
2   cups (400 grams) granulated sugar
6   large eggs (300 grams), room temperature
1   tablespoon (13 grams) vanilla extract
3   cups (375 grams) all-purpose flour
1   teaspoon (3 grams) kosher salt
½   teaspoon (2.5 grams) baking powder
1   cup (240 grams) whole milk, room temperature

1. Preheat oven to 325°F (170°C).
2. In the bowl of a stand mixer fitted with the paddle attachment, beat butter and sugar at medium speed until fluffy, 5 to 7 minutes, stopping to scrape sides of bowl. Reduce mixer speed to low, and add eggs, one at a time, beating well after each addition. Beat in vanilla.
3. In a medium bowl, whisk together flour, salt, and baking powder. With mixer on low speed, gradually add flour mixture to butter mixture alternately with milk, beginning and ending with flour mixture, beating just until combined after each addition.
4. Spray a 10-cup Bundt pan with baking spray with flour. Pour batter into prepared pan. Tap pan on a kitchen towel-lined counter a few times to settle batter and release any air bubbles.
5. Bake until a wooden pick inserted near center comes out clean, about 1 hour. Let cool in pan for 10 minutes. Invert cake onto a wire rack, and let cool completely.

FLAVOR VARIATIONS

Lemon Pound Cake:
Add 1 tablespoon (3 grams) lemon zest with butter and sugar; omit vanilla extract.

Almond Pound Cake:
Substitute 1½ teaspoons (6 grams) almond extract for vanilla extract.

BASQUE
BUNDT CAKE

Makes 1 (10-cup) Bundt cake

The gâteau Basque, a classic French cake filled with luxurious pastry cream, is one of my favorites. When I saw a loaf cake take on the menu at one of my favorite restaurants, Highlands Bar & Grill in Birmingham, Alabama, I was thrilled. When I tasted the cake, I found that rather than having a pastry cream filling, it had the cream mixed right into the batter, and I was inspired to take the innovation one step further with a beautiful Bundt cake. We made a Basque Custard that we then stirred into a plain pound cake base, creating a cake that tastes of pastry cream but has the texture of a tender pound cake.

1½   cups (340 grams) unsalted butter, softened
2   cups (400 grams) granulated sugar
5   large eggs (250 grams), room temperature
3   cups (375 grams) all-purpose flour
1   teaspoon (3 grams) kosher salt
½   teaspoon (1 gram) cream of tartar
1⅔   cups (360 grams) Basque Custard (recipe follows)
Confectioners' sugar, for dusting

1. Preheat oven to 350°F (180°C).
2. In the bowl of a stand mixer fitted with the paddle attachment, beat butter and granulated sugar at low speed just until combined; increase mixer speed to medium, and beat until fluffy, 3 to 4 minutes, stopping to scrape sides of bowl. Add eggs, one at time, beating well after each addition.
3. In a medium bowl, whisk together flour, salt, and cream of tartar. Gradually add flour mixture to butter mixture alternately with Basque Custard, beginning and ending with flour mixture, beating just until combined after each addition and stopping to scrape sides of bowl.
4. Spray a 10-cup Bundt pan with baking spray with flour. Spoon and spread batter evenly into prepared pan. Tap pan on a kitchen towel-lined counter a few times to settle batter and release any air bubbles.

5. Bake until golden brown and a wooden pick inserted in center comes out clean, 1 hour to 1 hour and 10 minutes, loosely covering with foil to prevent excess browning, if necessary. Let cool in pan for 10 minutes. Invert cake onto a wire rack. Serve warm or at room temperature. Dust with confectioners' sugar just before serving.

BASQUE CUSTARD
Makes about 2 cups

2   cups (480 grams) whole milk
1   vanilla bean, split lengthwise, seeds scraped and reserved
⅓   cup (67 grams) granulated sugar
⅓   cup (40 grams) cornstarch
2   tablespoons (15 grams) all-purpose flour
4   large egg yolks (74 grams)
1   large egg (50 grams)
½   teaspoon (1.5 grams) kosher salt

1. Place a fine-mesh sieve over a medium bowl.
2. In a medium saucepan, heat milk and reserved vanilla bean seeds over medium heat until steaming. (Do not boil.)
3. In a medium bowl, whisk together sugar, cornstarch, flour, egg yolks, egg, and salt. Gradually whisk hot milk mixture into sugar mixture. Return mixture to saucepan, and cook, whisking constantly, until bubbly and very thick, 2 to 6 minutes. Strain through prepared sieve. Cover with a piece of plastic wrap, pressing wrap directly onto surface of custard to prevent a skin from forming. Use warm.

PRO TIP
Any extra Basque Custard makes a great filling for stuffed French toast, mini tart shells, and more.

CHOCOLATE POUND CAKE WITH HOT FUDGE SAUCE

Makes 1 (15-cup) Bundt cake

The only thing that could improve this soft, delicate chocolate pound cake? A generous dollop of our homemade Hot Fudge Sauce.

1½   cups (340 grams) unsalted butter, softened
3   cups (600 grams) granulated sugar
5   large eggs (250 grams), room temperature
1   teaspoon (4 grams) vanilla extract
3   cups (375 grams) all-purpose flour
⅓   cup (25 grams) Dutch process cocoa powder
½   teaspoon (2.5 grams) baking soda
½   teaspoon (2.5 grams) baking powder
½   teaspoon (1.5 grams) kosher salt
¾   cup (180 grams) whole buttermilk, room temperature
½   cup (120 grams) sour cream, room temperature
Hot Fudge Sauce (recipe follows)
Garnish: confectioners' sugar

1. Preheat oven to 325°F (170°C).
2. In the bowl of a stand mixer fitted with the paddle attachment, beat butter and granulated sugar at medium speed until fluffy, 3 to 4 minutes, stopping to scrape sides of bowl. Add eggs, one at a time, beating well after each addition. Beat in vanilla.
3. In a medium bowl, whisk together flour, cocoa, baking soda, baking powder, and salt. With stand mixer on low speed, gradually add flour mixture to butter mixture alternately with buttermilk, beginning and ending with flour mixture, beating just until combined after each addition. Stir in sour cream.
4. Spray a 15-cup Bundt pan with baking spray with flour. Pour batter into prepared pan.
5. Bake until a wooden pick inserted near center comes out clean, about 1 hour. Let cool in pan for 10 minutes. Serve with Hot Fudge Sauce. Garnish with confectioners' sugar, if desired.

HOT FUDGE SAUCE

Makes about 2½ cups

3   ounces (85 grams) unsweetened chocolate, chopped
½   cup (113 grams) unsalted butter
1   cup (200 grams) granulated sugar
½   cup (110 grams) firmly packed light brown sugar
1   cup (240 grams) heavy whipping cream
1   teaspoon (4 grams) vanilla extract

1. In a medium saucepan, heat chocolate and butter over medium heat, stirring frequently, until melted and smooth. Stir in sugars. Add cream; bring to a boil over medium-high heat. Reduce heat, and simmer, stirring frequently, for 5 minutes. Remove from heat, and stir in vanilla. Cover and refrigerate for up to 1 week.

COCONUT BUNDT CAKE

Makes 1 (15-cup) Bundt cake

Say goodbye to your self-control. This Coconut Bundt Cake is everything you want and more in a pound cake.

1   cup (227 grams) unsalted butter, softened
2½   cups (500 grams) granulated sugar
4   large eggs (200 grams), room temperature
1½   teaspoons (6 grams) vanilla extract
3   cups (375 grams) all-purpose flour
1½   teaspoons (4.5 grams) kosher salt
1   teaspoon (5 grams) baking powder
1¼   cups (300 grams) unsweetened coconut milk, divided
2   cups (120 grams) sweetened flaked coconut
¼   cup (60 grams) sour cream, room temperature
¼   cup (60 grams) coconut cream
2   cups (240 grams) confectioners' sugar
3   tablespoons (45 grams) cream of coconut*
3   tablespoons (45 grams) whole milk
Garnish: sweetened flaked coconut

1. Preheat oven to 325°F (170°C).
2. In the bowl of a stand mixer fitted with the paddle attachment, beat butter and granulated sugar at medium speed until fluffy, 3 to 4 minutes, stopping to scrape sides of bowl. Add eggs, one at a time, beating just until combined after each addition. Beat in vanilla.
3. In a medium bowl, whisk together flour, salt, and baking powder. With mixer on low speed, gradually add flour mixture to butter mixture alternately with 1 cup (240 grams) coconut milk, beginning and ending with flour mixture, beating just until combined after each addition. Beat in flaked coconut and sour cream.

4. Spray a 15-cup Bundt pan with baking spray with flour. Spoon batter into prepared pan, smoothing top.
5. Bake until a wooden pick inserted in center comes out clean, about 1 hour and 20 minutes.
6. Meanwhile, in a small saucepan, heat coconut cream and remaining ¼ cup (60 grams) coconut milk over medium-high heat, stirring until smooth. Let cool to room temperature.
7. Using a wooden pick or skewer, poke holes in warm cake. Gradually pour coconut cream mixture over top of cake. Let cool in pan for 20 minutes.
8. Line a rimmed baking sheet with foil; place a wire rack on prepared pan. Invert cake onto wire rack, and let cool completely.
9. In a small bowl, whisk together confectioners' sugar and cream of coconut. Stir in milk, 1 teaspoon (5 grams) at a time, until desired consistency is reached. Drizzle glaze onto cooled cake. Garnish with flaked coconut, if desired.

*We used Coco Lopez.

ALMOND POPPY SEED BUNDT CAKE

Makes 1 (10-cup) Bundt cake

This cake switches the classic lemon and poppy seed pairing by subbing in almond extract for a sweet flavor upgrade.

1½	cups (340 grams) unsalted butter, softened
3	cups (600 grams) granulated sugar
2	teaspoons (8 grams) vanilla extract
2	teaspoons (8 grams) almond extract
5	large eggs (250 grams)
3	cups (375 grams) all-purpose flour
1	teaspoon (3 grams) kosher salt
½	teaspoon (2.5 grams) baking powder
1	cup (240 grams) whole buttermilk
2	tablespoons (18 grams) poppy seeds

1. Preheat oven to 325°F (170°C).

2. In the bowl of a stand mixer fitted with the paddle attachment, beat butter, granulated sugar, and extracts at medium speed until fluffy, 3 to 4 minutes, stopping to scrape sides of bowl. Add eggs, one at a time, beating well after each addition.

3. In a medium bowl, whisk together flour, salt, and baking powder. With mixer on low speed, gradually add flour mixture to butter mixture alternately with buttermilk, beginning and ending with flour mixture, beating just until combined after each addition. Gently stir in poppy seeds.

4. Spray a 10-cup Bundt pan with baking spray with flour. Spoon batter into prepared pan, smoothing top with a small offset spatula. Run a knife through batter to release any air bubbles.

5. Bake until a wooden pick inserted near center comes out clean, about 1 hour and 15 minutes. Let cool in pan for 15 minutes. Invert onto a wire rack, and let cool completely.

PRO TIP
Inverting the cake onto a wire rack and letting it cool in the pan allows gravity to help release the cake. To check if the cake has released, gently shift the Bundt pan side to side while inverted on the wire rack; if it moves freely, the cake has let go.

CLASSIC POUND CAKE

Makes 1 (15-cup) Bundt cake

Dense and decadent, this elegant yet simple recipe transforms butter, flour, sugar, and eggs into slices of perfection.

1½ cups (340 grams) unsalted butter, softened
3   cups (600 grams) granulated sugar
7   large eggs (350 grams), room temperature
1½ teaspoons (6 grams) vanilla extract
3   cups (375 grams) all-purpose flour
¼   teaspoon (1 gram) kosher salt
1   cup (240 grams) heavy whipping cream, room temperature
Garnish: confectioners' sugar

1. Preheat oven to 300°F (150°C).
2. In the bowl of a stand mixer fitted with the paddle attachment, beat butter and granulated sugar at medium speed until fluffy, 6 to 7 minutes, stopping to scrape sides of bowl. Add eggs, one at a time, beating well after each addition. Beat in vanilla.
3. In a medium bowl, sift together flour and salt. Gradually add flour mixture to butter mixture alternately with cream, beginning and ending with flour mixture, beating just until combined after each addition.

4. Spray a 15-cup Bundt pan with baking spray with flour. Spoon batter into prepared pan.
5. Bake for 1 hour. Loosely cover with foil, and bake until a wooden pick inserted near center comes out clean, 45 to 55 minutes more. Let cool in pan for 15 minutes. Invert cake onto a wire rack, and let cool completely. Garnish with confectioners' sugar, if desired.

TRES LECHES POUND CAKE

Makes 1 (15-cup) Bundt cake

We transformed this Latin American dessert into a dense pound cake, made with three milks, of course.

2   cups (454 grams) unsalted butter, softened
3   cups plus 2 tablespoons (624 grams) granulated sugar, divided
6   large eggs (300 grams), room temperature
3   teaspoons (12 grams) vanilla extract, divided
4½   cups (563 grams) all-purpose flour
½   teaspoon (1.5 grams) kosher salt
1   (14-ounce) can (397 grams) sweetened condensed milk
½   cup (120 grams) whole milk
¼   cup (60 grams) water
1   cup (240 grams) heavy whipping cream
Garnish: confectioners' sugar

1. Preheat oven to 300°F (150°C).
2. In the bowl of a stand mixer fitted with the paddle attachment, beat butter and 2 cups (400 grams) granulated sugar at medium speed until creamy, 3 to 4 minutes, stopping to scrape sides of bowl. Add eggs, one at a time, beating well after each addition. Beat in 2 teaspoons (8 grams) vanilla.
3. In a large bowl, whisk together flour and salt. In a medium bowl, whisk together condensed milk and whole milk. With mixer on low speed, gradually add flour mixture to butter mixture alternately with milk mixture, beginning and ending with flour mixture, beating just until combined after each addition.
4. Spray a 15-cup Bundt pan with baking spray with flour. Pour batter into prepared pan.

5. Bake until a wooden pick inserted near center comes out clean, about 1½ hours, covering with foil after 45 minutes of baking to prevent excess browning.
6. Meanwhile, in a small saucepan, bring ¼ cup (60 grams) water and remaining 1 cup plus 2 tablespoons (224 grams) granulated sugar to a boil over medium-high heat. Remove from heat. Gradually whisk in cream and remaining 1 teaspoon (4 grams) vanilla. Let cool completely.
7. Using a wooden pick or skewer, poke holes in warm cake in pan. Slowly pour 1 cup sugar mixture over top of cake in pan. Let cool for 30 minutes. Invert cake onto a wire rack lined with foil. Poke holes in cake, and pour remaining sugar mixture over cake. Let cool completely. Garnish with confectioners' sugar, if desired. Refrigerate in an airtight container for up to 2 days.

ULTIMATE CREAM CHEESE-VANILLA BEAN POUND CAKE

Makes 1 (10-cup) Bundt cake

A delectable classic through and through, this recipe harnesses the decadent power of cream cheese to create a golden-crumbed pound cake. With a vanilla-forward flavor, all this dessert needs for decoration is a light dusting of confectioners' sugar.

8	ounces (226 grams) cream cheese, room temperature
¾	cup (170 grams) unsalted butter, softened
2	cups (400 grams) granulated sugar
4	large eggs (200 grams), room temperature
1	vanilla bean, split lengthwise, seeds scraped and reserved
1	tablespoon (13 grams) vanilla extract
2½	cups (313 grams) all-purpose flour
1	teaspoon (5 grams) baking powder
½	teaspoon (1.5 grams) kosher salt
¾	cup (180 grams) heavy whipping cream, room temperature

Garnish: confectioners' sugar

1. Preheat oven to 325°F (170°C).

2. In the bowl of a stand mixer fitted with the paddle attachment, beat cream cheese and butter at medium speed until creamy. Add granulated sugar; beat until fluffy, 3 to 4 minutes, stopping to scrape sides of bowl. Add eggs, one at a time, beating well after each addition. Beat in reserved vanilla bean seeds and vanilla extract.

3. In a large bowl, whisk together flour, baking powder, and salt. With mixer on low speed, gradually add flour mixture to butter mixture alternately with cream, beginning and ending with flour mixture, beating just until combined after each addition.

4. Spray a 10-cup Bundt pan with baking spray with flour. Spoon batter into prepared pan.

5. Bake until a wooden pick inserted near center comes out clean, 1 hour and 20 minutes to 1½ hours, covering with foil halfway through baking to prevent excess browning. Let cool in pan for 10 minutes. Invert cake onto a wire rack, and let cool completely. Garnish with confectioners' sugar, if desired.

PRO TIP

When you're incorporating cream cheese into a filling, dough, or anything else, always make sure it is at room temperature. Cream cheese, like butter, is hard to whip when cold because its milk fat is still firm and solid. Chilled cream cheese, when mixed with other, more liquid ingredients, will take on a curdled appearance. Leave your cream cheese out at room temperature for at least 4 hours (or even overnight) before using in your recipe.

ITALIAN CREAM BUNDT CAKE

Makes 1 (15-cup) Bundt cake

This cake delivers the same flavors as its three-layered cousin in a supermoist, confectioners' sugar-dusted package. It's Italian cream cake simplified.

1½   cups (340 grams) unsalted butter, softened
8   ounces (226 grams) cream cheese, softened
2   cups (400 grams) granulated sugar
1   cup (220 grams) firmly packed light brown sugar
1½   teaspoons (4.5 grams) kosher salt
5   large eggs (250 grams), room temperature
1   tablespoon (13 grams) vanilla extract
3   cups (375 grams) all-purpose flour
½   teaspoon (2.5 grams) baking powder
1   cup (113 grams) finely chopped toasted pecans
1   cup (60 grams) sweetened flaked coconut, toasted
Garnish: confectioners' sugar

1. In the bowl of a stand mixer fitted with the paddle attachment, beat butter and cream cheese at medium speed until creamy, 3 to 4 minutes. Increase mixer speed to high, and add granulated sugar, brown sugar, and salt; beat for 10 minutes, stopping to scrape sides of bowl. Add eggs, one at a time, beating well after each addition. Beat in vanilla.

2. In a medium bowl, whisk together flour and baking powder. With mixer on low speed, gradually add flour mixture to butter mixture, beating until combined. Beat in pecans and coconut.

3. Spray a 15-cup Bundt pan with baking spray with flour. Spoon batter into prepared pan.

4. Place pan in a cold oven. Bake at 300°F (150°C) until a wooden pick inserted near center comes out clean, about 1 hour and 20 minutes. Let cool in pan for 10 minutes. Invert cake onto a wire rack, and let cool completely. Garnish with confectioners' sugar, if desired.

BIRTHDAY CAKE BUNDT

Makes 1 (10-cup) Bundt cake

It's time to celebrate! This sprinkle-packed Bundt cake is heavy on the vanilla and festive fun, making it the perfect addition to your birthday party—or any other celebration.

½ cup (113 grams) unsalted butter, softened
1½ cups (300 grams) granulated sugar
2 large eggs (100 grams), room temperature
2 teaspoons (8 grams) vanilla extract
¾ teaspoon (3 grams) almond extract
2½ cups (313 grams) all-purpose flour
4 teaspoons (20 grams) baking powder
½ teaspoon (1.5 grams) kosher salt
1 cup (240 grams) whole buttermilk, room temperature
½ cup (96 grams) rainbow sprinkles*
Vanilla Almond Glaze (recipe follows)
Garnish: rainbow sprinkles

1. Preheat oven to 325°F (170°C).
2. In the bowl of a stand mixer fitted with the paddle attachment, beat butter and sugar at medium speed until fluffy, 3 to 4 minutes, stopping to scrape sides of bowl. Add eggs, one at time, beating well after each addition. Beat in extracts.
3. In a medium bowl, whisk together flour, baking powder, and salt. With mixer on low speed, gradually add flour mixture to butter mixture alternately with buttermilk, beating just until combined after each addition. Stir in sprinkles.
4. Spray a 10-cup Bundt pan with baking spray with flour. Pour batter into prepared pan, smoothing top, if necessary. Tap pan on a kitchen towel-lined counter a few times to settle batter and release any air bubbles.

5. Bake until a wooden pick inserted near center comes out clean, 55 minutes to 1 hour. Let cool in pan for 15 minutes. Invert cake onto a wire rack, and let cool completely. Spoon Vanilla Almond Glaze onto cooled cake. Garnish with sprinkles.

*We used Betty Crocker Rainbow Sprinkles.

Vanilla Almond Glaze
Makes ¾ cup

2 cups (240 grams) confectioners' sugar
3 tablespoons (45 grams) whole milk
1 teaspoon (4 grams) vanilla extract
½ teaspoon (2 grams) almond extract

1. In a medium bowl, whisk together all ingredients until smooth.

PRO TIP
When baking in an ultra-detailed Bundt cake pan, spray thoroughly with baking spray with flour so the cake comes out cleanly from every nook and cranny.

SPICE
IS NICE

RICH WITH CARDAMOM,
CINNAMON, ALLSPICE,
AND MORE, EACH OF THESE
BUNDT CAKES MAKES THE
MOST OF YOUR FAVORITE
INGREDIENTS ON THE
SPICE RACK

EASY SPICED SWIRL BUNDT CAKE

Makes 1 (15-cup) Bundt cake

Packed with a tight spiral of aromatic spices and brown sugar, this simple cake can be pulled together quickly for a fuss-free and fun dessert.

1½   cups (340 grams) unsalted butter, softened
1½   cups (300 grams) granulated sugar
1   cup (220 grams) firmly packed light brown sugar
4   large eggs (200 grams), room temperature
2   teaspoons (8 grams) vanilla extract
4   cups (500 grams) all-purpose flour
2½   teaspoons (12.5 grams) baking powder
½   teaspoon (1.5 grams) kosher salt
1½   cups (360 grams) sour cream,
     room temperature
Sugared Spice Blend (recipe follows)
2   cups (240 grams) confectioners' sugar
3   tablespoons (45 grams) whole milk
2   tablespoons (28 grams) light corn syrup

1. Preheat oven to 325°F (170°C).
2. In the bowl of a stand mixer fitted with the paddle attachment, beat butter, granulated sugar, and brown sugar at medium speed until fluffy, 3 to 4 minutes, stopping to scrape sides of bowl. Add eggs, one at a time, beating well after each addition. Beat in vanilla.
3. In a large bowl, whisk together flour, baking powder, and salt. With mixer on low speed, gradually add flour mixture to butter mixture alternately with sour cream, beginning and ending with flour mixture, beating just until combined after each addition.
4. Spray a 15-cup Bundt pan with baking spray with flour. Pour one-third of batter into prepared pan. Sprinkle with half of Sugared Spice Blend. Repeat layers once; top with remaining one-third of batter. Using a knife, swirl layers together.
5. Bake until a wooden pick inserted near center comes out clean, about 1 hour and 20 minutes. Let cool in pan for 10 minutes. Invert cake onto a wire rack, and let cool completely.
6. In a medium bowl, whisk together confectioners' sugar, milk, and corn syrup. Drizzle onto cooled cake.

SUGARED SPICE BLEND
Makes about ½ cup

½   cup (110 grams) firmly packed light brown sugar
2   teaspoons (4 grams) ground cinnamon
2   teaspoons (4 grams) ground cardamom
1   teaspoon (2 grams) ground cloves
1   teaspoon (2 grams) ground ginger
½   teaspoon (1 gram) ground white pepper

1. In a small bowl, stir together all ingredients until combined.

PAIN D'ÉPICE

Makes 1 (10-cup) Bundt cake

Recipe by Marjorie Taylor and Kendall Smith Franchini

Pain d'épice, or spice bread, is a classic Burgundian favorite. Traditionally, it is baked in a loaf pan, but Marjorie Taylor and Kendall Smith Franchini, founders of The Cook's Atelier in Beaune, France, like to make theirs a bit more festive by baking it in a fluted cake pan.

2   large eggs (100 grams), room temperature
1   cup (336 grams) honey
¾   cup (180 grams) water
½   cup (110 grams) firmly packed light brown sugar
2   cups (250 grams) unbleached all-purpose flour, divided
1½ teaspoons (7.5 grams) baking powder
½   teaspoon (2.5 grams) baking soda
1   teaspoon (2 grams) ground cinnamon
1   teaspoon (2 grams) ground nutmeg
1   teaspoon (2 grams) ground ginger
1   teaspoon (2 grams) ground coriander
1   teaspoon (2 grams) ground aniseed
½   teaspoon (1 gram) ground cloves
¼   teaspoon ground black pepper
1   tablespoon (3 grams) lemon zest
1   tablespoon (3 grams) orange zest
Pinch fleur de sel
Garnish: confectioners' sugar

1. Preheat oven to 350°F (180°C).

2. In a large bowl, whisk eggs.

3. In a large saucepan, combine honey, ¾ cup (180 grams) water, and brown sugar, and bring to a boil. Remove from heat, and sift 1 cup (125 grams) flour over mixture, whisking vigorously.

4. In a large bowl, sift together baking powder, baking soda, cinnamon, nutmeg, ginger, coriander, aniseed, cloves, pepper, and remaining 1 cup (125 grams) flour. Add lemon zest, orange zest, and fleur de sel.

5. Slowly add honey mixture to eggs, whisking constantly. Gradually add baking powder mixture to egg mixture, whisking constantly to avoid any lumps.

6. Spray a 10-cup Bundt pan with baking spray with flour. Pour batter into prepared pan.

7. Bake until firm to the touch, 35 to 40 minutes. Let cool in pan for 10 minutes. Invert cake onto a wire rack, and let cool completely. Garnish with confectioners' sugar, if desired.

Photo by Joann Pai

PRO TIP

Fleur de sel has snowflake-like crystals that have been gently raked from the tops of solar-evaporated seawater ponds. Because of the large flakes, a little goes a long way. In a pinch, Maldon sea salt flakes will work as well.

SPICED SWEET POTATO BUNDT CAKE

Makes 1 (15-cup) Bundt cake

Shredded sweet potato studs this delicious pumpkin pie spice-packed Bundt cake.

¾	cup (170 grams) unsalted butter, softened
8	ounces (226 grams) cream cheese, softened
1	cup (200 grams) granulated sugar
1	cup (220 grams) firmly packed light brown sugar
4	large eggs (200 grams), room temperature
1½	cups (225 grams) shredded peeled sweet potato
1½	teaspoons (6 grams) vanilla extract, divided
3	cups (375 grams) self-rising flour (see Note)
1	teaspoon (2 grams) pumpkin pie spice
1	teaspoon (2.25 grams) kosher salt, divided
1½	cups (180 grams) confectioners' sugar
2½	tablespoons (37.5 grams) whole buttermilk
1	tablespoon (14 grams) unsalted butter, melted

Garnish: chopped toasted pecans

1. Preheat oven to 350°F (180°C).
2. In the bowl of a stand mixer fitted with the paddle attachment, beat butter and cream cheese at medium speed until creamy, 1 to 2 minutes. Add granulated sugar and brown sugar, and beat until fluffy, 2 to 3 minutes, stopping to scrape sides of bowl. Add eggs, one at a time, beating well after each addition. Add sweet potato and 1 teaspoon (4 grams) vanilla, beating until combined.
3. In a medium bowl, whisk together flour, pie spice, and ¾ teaspoon (2.25 grams) salt. With mixer on low speed, gradually add flour mixture to butter mixture, beating just until combined.

4. Spray a 15-cup Bundt pan with baking spray with flour. Spoon batter into prepared pan. Tap pan on a kitchen towel-lined counter a few times to settle batter and release any air bubbles.
5. Bake until a wooden pick inserted near center comes out clean, 40 to 45 minutes. Let cool in pan for 10 minutes. Invert cake onto a wire rack, and let cool completely.
6. In a medium bowl, whisk together confectioners' sugar, buttermilk, melted butter, remaining ½ teaspoon (2 grams) vanilla, and remaining ¼ teaspoon salt until smooth. Spoon onto cooled cake. Garnish with pecans, if desired. Store in an airtight container for up to 3 days.

Note: *Self-rising flour is made up of a combination of all-purpose flour, baking powder, and salt. To make your own, for every 1 cup (125 grams) all-purpose flour, add 1½ teaspoons (12 grams) baking powder and 1 teaspoon (3 grams) kosher salt.*

CHAI BUTTERNUT SQUASH BUNDT CAKE

Makes 1 (10-cup) Bundt cake

The chai flavor in this cake is very soft and enhances the natural sweetness of the butternut squash.

1 tablespoon (6 grams) loose-leaf chai tea
8 ounces (226 grams) cream cheese, softened
2⅔ cups (533 grams) granulated sugar, divided
4 large eggs (200 grams), room temperature and divided
2¾ cups (344 grams) plus 1 tablespoon (8 grams) all-purpose flour, divided
1 cup (227 grams) unsalted butter, softened
1 teaspoon (4 grams) vanilla extract
1 teaspoon (5 grams) baking soda
1 teaspoon (3 grams) kosher salt
1 cup (220 grams) mashed cooked butternut squash
½ cup (120 grams) whole milk, room temperature
1 tablespoon (3 grams) orange zest
Walnut Syrup (recipe follows)

1. In the container of a blender or spice grinder, place loose tea; blend until finely ground, about 1 minute. Set aside.
2. In the bowl of a stand mixer fitted with the paddle attachment, beat cream cheese at medium speed until creamy, 2 to 3 minutes. Add ⅔ cup (133 grams) sugar, and beat until combined. Add 1 egg (50 grams) and 1 tablespoon (8 grams) flour, and beat until smooth. Place cream cheese mixture in a large pastry bag, and cut a ½-inch opening in tip. Set aside.
3. Preheat oven to 325°F (170°C).
4. Clean bowl of stand mixer and paddle attachment. Using the paddle attachment, beat butter, vanilla, and remaining 2 cups (400 grams) sugar with a mixer at medium speed until fluffy, 4 to 5 minutes, stopping to scrape sides of bowl. Add remaining 3 eggs (150 grams), one at a time, beating well after each addition.

5. In a medium bowl, whisk together ground tea, baking soda, salt, and remaining 2¾ cups (344 grams) flour. In another medium bowl, combine mashed squash, milk, and orange zest. With mixer on low speed, gradually add tea mixture to butter mixture alternately with squash mixture, beginning and ending with tea mixture, beating just until combined after each addition.
6. Spray a 10-cup Bundt pan with baking spray with flour. Spoon three-fourths of batter into prepared pan. Make a deep well in center of batter with the back of a spoon. Pipe cream cheese mixture into well. Gently spoon remaining batter on top, spreading until smooth.
7. Bake until a wooden pick inserted near center comes out with a few moist crumbs, about 1 hour. Let cool in pan for 10 minutes. Invert cake onto a wire rack, and let cool completely. Serve with Walnut Syrup.

WALNUT SYRUP
Makes about 1½ cups

½ cup (170 grams) light corn syrup
½ cup (170 grams) maple syrup
1 cup (113 grams) coarsely chopped walnuts
2 tablespoons (28 grams) unsalted butter
1 teaspoon (4 grams) vanilla extract

1. In a small saucepan, bring corn syrup and maple syrup to a boil over medium-high heat. Remove from heat; stir in walnuts, butter, and vanilla. Serve immediately.

APPLE-CINNAMON SUGAR DOUGHNUT BUNDT CAKE

Makes 1 (10-cup) Bundt cake

Cider gives this cake its robust apple flavor. To get the full effect, be sure to reduce the cider until it is thick like syrup.

6   cups (1,440 grams) apple cider
1   cup (227 grams) unsalted butter, softened
1¼   cups (250 grams) granulated sugar, divided
3   large eggs (150 grams), room temperature
1   teaspoon (4 grams) vanilla extract
3¼   cups (406 grams) all-purpose flour
2   tablespoons (12 grams) ground cinnamon, divided
2   teaspoons (6 grams) kosher salt
1   teaspoon (5 grams) baking powder
½   teaspoon (2.5 grams) baking soda
½   cup (120 grams) whole milk, room temperature
1   teaspoon (5 grams) apple cider vinegar
1   large McIntosh apple (185 grams), peeled and chopped
⅔   cup (80 grams) confectioners' sugar
1   tablespoon (15 grams) water

1. In a large saucepan, bring cider to a boil over medium-high heat. Cook until cider is reduced to 1½ cups, about 1½ hours, stirring frequently during last 30 minutes. Remove from heat; let cool completely.

2. Preheat oven to 325°F (170°C).

3. In the bowl of a stand mixer fitted with the paddle attachment, beat butter and 1 cup (200 grams) granulated sugar at medium speed until creamy, 3 to 4 minutes, stopping to scrape sides of bowl. Add eggs, one at a time, beating well after each addition. Beat in vanilla.

4. In a medium bowl, whisk together flour, 1 tablespoon (6 grams) cinnamon, salt, baking powder, and baking soda. In a small bowl, stir together reduced cider, milk, and vinegar. With mixer on low speed, gradually add flour mixture to butter mixture alternately with cider mixture, beginning and ending with flour mixture, beating just until combined after each addition. Stir in apple.

5. Spray a 10-cup Bundt pan with baking spray with flour. Pour batter into prepared pan.

6. Bake until a wooden pick inserted near center comes out with a few moist crumbs, about 1 hour. Let cool in pan for 10 minutes. Invert cake onto a wire rack, and let cool for 30 minutes.

7. In a small bowl, whisk together confectioners' sugar and 1 tablespoon (15 grams) water until smooth. Brush mixture onto cake, working quickly to keep moist.

8. In another small bowl, combine remaining ¼ cup (50 grams) granulated sugar and remaining 1 tablespoon (6 grams) cinnamon; sprinkle onto cake. Serve warm or at room temperature.

SPICED COCONUT OIL CAKE WITH BOURBON GLAZE

Makes 1 (15-cup) Bundt cake

Recipe by Julie Tanous and Jesse Tyler Ferguson

Julie and Jesse love baking with coconut oil and try to substitute it for butter whenever possible. Both fans of Indian cuisine, the two added lots of aromatic spices—ginger, cardamom, and nutmeg—to this moist cake. Topped with nutty pecans and a sugary glaze with sweet bourbon (one of their favorite spirits), it features all the warmth of the holiday season.

3	cups (375 grams) all-purpose flour
2	teaspoons (4 grams) ground allspice
2	teaspoons (4 grams) ground ginger
1½	teaspoons (3 grams) ground cinnamon
1½	teaspoons (3 grams) ground nutmeg
1¼	teaspoons (2.5 grams) ground cloves
1	teaspoon (5 grams) baking powder
1	teaspoon (3 grams) kosher salt
1	teaspoon (2 grams) ground cardamom
½	teaspoon (2.5 grams) baking soda
1	cup (240 grams) whole buttermilk, room temperature
½	cup (170 grams) molasses
2	teaspoons (8 grams) vanilla extract
2⅓	cups (467 grams) granulated sugar
1	cup (238 grams) coconut oil, room temperature, plus more for greasing the pan
4	large eggs (200 grams)
2	cups (226 grams) chopped pecans, divided
2	cups (432 grams) confectioners' sugar
7	tablespoons (85 grams) heavy whipping cream
2	tablespoons (30 grams) bourbon
⅓	cup (38 grams) roughly chopped pecans

1. Preheat oven to 325°F (170°C).

2. In a medium bowl, whisk together flour, allspice, ginger, cinnamon, nutmeg, cloves, baking powder, salt, cardamom, and baking soda. Set aside.

3. In a small bowl, whisk together buttermilk, molasses, and vanilla until combined; set aside.

4. In the bowl of a stand mixer fitted with the paddle attachment, beat sugar and coconut oil at medium-high speed until fluffy, about 3 minutes. Add eggs, one at a time, beating until combined after each addition. Beat until light and very fluffy, about 4 minutes, stopping to scrape sides and bottom of bowl.

5. With mixer on low speed, add flour mixture in two additions alternately with buttermilk mixture, beginning and ending with flour mixture, beating just until combined after each addition and stopping to scrape sides of bowl. (Do not overmix.) Fold in 1 cup (113 grams) chopped pecans.

6. Grease a 15-cup Bundt pan with coconut oil, and lightly flour. Sprinkle ½ cup (56.5 grams) chopped pecans in bottom of prepared pan. Pour batter over pecans in pan, smoothing top with an offset spatula. Sprinkle remaining ½ cup (56.5 grams) chopped pecans evenly on top of batter.

7. Bake until golden brown and a wooden pick inserted near center comes out clean, 55 minutes to 1 hour and 5 minutes. Let cool in pan for 10 minutes. Invert cake onto a wire rack, and let cool completely.

8. In a medium bowl, whisk together confectioners' sugar, cream, and bourbon. Drizzle onto cooled cake, and sprinkle with roughly chopped pecans.

Photo by Matt Armendariz, Food Styling by Marian Cooper Cairns

SNICKERDOODLE SWIRL BUNDT CAKE WITH SALTED PISTACHIOS

Makes 1 (10-cup) Bundt cake

The classic cookie favorite gets a Bundt cake spin. Enhanced with salty, crunchy pistachios and bursting with robust cinnamon flavor, this Bundt offers all of the cookie's pleasures in a beautiful cake package.

4   cups (500 grams) self-rising flour
1½   cups (300 grams) granulated sugar, divided
1   teaspoon (3 grams) kosher salt
1½   cups (360 grams) whole milk, room temperature
½   cup (112 grams) vegetable oil
2   large eggs (100 grams), room temperature
1   tablespoon (6 grams) ground cinnamon
1   cup (112 grams) chopped roasted salted pistachios, divided

1. Preheat oven to 325°F (150°C).
2. In a medium bowl, whisk together flour, 1 cup (200 grams) sugar, and salt. Add milk, oil, and eggs, whisking to combine.
3. In a small bowl, stir together cinnamon and remaining ½ cup (100 grams) sugar.
4. Spray a 10-cup Bundt pan with baking spray with flour. Add ½ cup (56 grams) pistachios to pan, and swirl to lightly coat pan, leaving larger nuts in bottom of pan. Spread one-fourth of batter in prepared pan. Sprinkle with half of cinnamon sugar. Top with ¼ cup (28 grams) pistachios. Spoon one-fourth of batter onto pistachios in pan; sprinkle remaining cinnamon sugar on top of batter, and top with remaining ¼ cup (28 grams) pistachios. Spoon remaining batter on top.
5. Bake until a wooden pick inserted near center comes out clean, 45 to 50 minutes, covering with foil halfway through baking to prevent excess browning. Let cool in pan for 10 minutes. Invert onto a wire rack, and let cool completely.

SPICED BUNDT CAKE

Makes 1 (10-cup) Bundt cake

*This delicately spiced Bundt cake is made tender with applesauce,
making it the perfect fall season treat.*

2	cups (250 grams) self-rising flour
1	cup (200 grams) granulated sugar
1	tablespoon (6 grams) ground cinnamon
2	teaspoons (4 grams) ground cloves
1	cup (224 grams) vegetable oil
3	large eggs (150 grams), room temperature
⅓	cup (80 grams) applesauce

Garnish: confectioners' sugar

1. Preheat oven to 350°F (180°C).
2. In the bowl of a stand mixer fitted with the paddle attachment,
whisk together flour, granulated sugar, cinnamon, and cloves. Add
oil, eggs, and applesauce. Beat at low speed until combined, about
1 minute. (Batter will be thin.)
3. Spray a 10-cup Bundt pan with baking spray with flour. Pour
batter into prepared pan. Tap pan on a kitchen towel-lined counter
a few times to settle batter and release any air bubbles.
4. Bake until a wooden pick inserted near center comes out clean,
35 to 40 minutes. Let cool in pan for 10 minutes. Invert cake onto
a wire rack, and let cool completely. Garnish with confectioners'
sugar, if desired.

GINGERBREAD BUNDT CAKE WITH BUTTERMILK GLAZE

Makes 1 (10-cup) Bundt cake

With roots in Europe—most famously in Germany, where every home has its own recipe—gingerbread varies from spicy to sugary sweet. This one includes a glossy coating of Buttermilk Glaze, which delicately balances the piquancy of the flavors within.

1	cup (227 grams) unsalted butter, softened
1¾	cups (385 grams) firmly packed dark brown sugar
2	teaspoons (5 grams) tightly packed lemon zest
2	large eggs (100 grams), room temperature
1	large egg yolk (19 grams), room temperature
⅔	cup (226 grams) molasses (not blackstrap)
3	cups (375 grams) unbleached cake flour
1	tablespoon (6 grams) ground ginger
2	teaspoons (10 grams) baking powder
2	teaspoons (4 grams) ground cinnamon
1¼	teaspoons (2.5 grams) ground nutmeg
¾	teaspoon (2.25 grams) kosher salt
½	teaspoon (1 gram) ground cloves
½	teaspoon (1 gram) ground allspice
¼	teaspoon (1.25 grams) baking soda
1¼	cups (300 grams) brewed coffee, room temperature

Buttermilk Glaze (recipe follows)
Garnish: sugared fresh cranberries, sugared fresh rosemary (see Note)

1. Preheat oven to 350°F (180°C).
2. In the bowl of a stand mixer fitted with the paddle attachment, beat butter, brown sugar, and lemon zest at medium-low speed just until combined. Increase mixer speed to medium, and beat until fluffy, 3 to 4 minutes, stopping to scrape sides of bowl. Add eggs and egg yolk, one at a time, beating until well combined after each addition. Beat in molasses. (Mixture may look slightly curdled at this point, but batter will come together.)

3. In a large bowl, whisk together flour, ginger, baking powder, cinnamon, nutmeg, salt, cloves, allspice, and baking soda. Add flour mixture to butter mixture alternately with coffee, beginning and ending with flour mixture, beating just until combined after each addition.
4. Spray a 10-cup Bundt pan with baking spray with flour. Spoon batter into prepared pan. Tap pan on a kitchen towel-lined counter a few times to settle batter and release any air bubbles.
5. Bake until a wooden pick inserted near center comes out clean, 50 minutes to 1 hour. Let cool in pan for 10 minutes. Using a small offset spatula, gently loosen center of cake. Invert cake onto a wire rack, and let cool completely.
6. Transfer cooled cake to a serving plate; spoon and spread Buttermilk Glaze on top. Garnish with sugared cranberries and rosemary, if desired.

Note: *To make sugared cranberries and rosemary, combine ½ cup (100 grams) granulated sugar and ½ cup (120 grams) water in a medium saucepan. Bring to a boil, and cook, stirring occasionally, until sugar dissolves; remove from heat, and let cool to room temperature. Working in batches, dip cranberries and rosemary in sugar syrup, coating thoroughly; let stand on a wire rack placed over a large rimmed baking sheet for 45 minutes. Dip cranberries and rosemary in sanding sugar, coating well on all sides and shaking off excess. Use immediately.*

BUTTERMILK GLAZE

Makes about ⅔ cup

1½	cups (180 grams) confectioners' sugar, sifted
2½	tablespoons (37.5 grams) whole buttermilk
1	tablespoon (14 grams) unsalted butter, melted
½	teaspoon (2 grams) vanilla extract
¼	teaspoon kosher salt

1. In a medium bowl, stir together all ingredients until smooth and well combined. Use immediately.

A YEAR OF BUNDTS

SHOWCASING A BUNDT FOR
EVERY MONTH, THIS CHAPTER
WILL TAKE YOU FROM
JANUARY'S CELEBRATORY
MIMOSA-INSPIRED
BUNDT TO DECEMBER'S
HOLIDAY-READY RED
VELVET STUNNER

JANUARY

MIMOSA
BUNDT CAKE

Makes 1 (6-cup) Bundt cake

Pop a cork and celebrate the new year with a Mimosa Bundt Cake! Packed with a double dose of orange zest and juice and a splash of Champagne, this Bundt has all the flavors of a mimosa in cake form. Baking it in a 6-cup Bundt pan yields a petite Bundt that's perfect for an intimate New Year's Day party. Topped with a Champagne-Orange Glaze and glamorous metallic sprinkles and glitter, this Mimosa Bundt Cake is a dessert worth toasting to.

1½ cups (300 grams) granulated sugar, divided
1½ cups (336 grams) Champagne or dry sparkling white wine, divided
1 tablespoon (6 grams) packed orange zest
¾ cup (168 grams) canola oil
3 large eggs (150 grams), room temperature
2 teaspoons (8 grams) vanilla extract
2¼ cups (281 grams) unbleached cake flour
1¾ teaspoons (8.75 grams) baking powder
¾ teaspoon (2.25 grams) kosher salt
¼ cup (60 grams) fresh orange juice
Champagne-Orange Glaze (recipe follows)
Edible gold glitter, for sprinkling
Garnish: assorted gold and silver sprinkles

1. Preheat oven to 350°F (180°C).
2. In a small saucepan, combine ¼ cup (50 grams) sugar and ¼ cup (56 grams) Champagne; cook over medium heat, stirring occasionally, until sugar dissolves, about 2 minutes. Remove from heat; transfer sugar mixture to a small bowl. Stir in ¾ cup (168 grams) Champagne; set aside.
3. In the bowl of a stand mixer fitted with the paddle attachment, beat orange zest and remaining 1¼ cups (250 grams) sugar at medium-low speed until fragrant and well combined, 30 seconds to 1 minute. Add oil, eggs, and vanilla; beat at medium speed until well combined, 1 to 2 minutes, stopping to scrape sides of bowl.
4. In a medium bowl, whisk together flour, baking powder, and salt. In a small bowl, stir together orange juice and remaining ½ cup (112 grams) Champagne. Add flour mixture to zest mixture alternately with juice mixture, beginning and ending with flour mixture, beating just until smooth and combined.
5. Spray a 6-cup Bundt pan with baking spray with flour. Pour batter into prepared pan. Tap pan on a kitchen towel-lined counter a few times to settle batter and release any air bubbles. (Pan will be quite full, but batter will not overflow during baking.)
6. Bake until a wooden pick inserted near center comes out clean, 35 to 40 minutes, loosely covering with foil to prevent excess browning, if necessary. Let cool in pan for 15 minutes. Using a small offset spatula, loosen cake from center of pan. Invert pan onto a wire rack; let cake cool in pan for 5 minutes. Remove pan.
7. Line a rimmed baking sheet with parchment paper. Spray a wire rack with cooking spray, and place on prepared pan.
8. Pour about half of reserved sugar mixture into Bundt pan. Carefully return cake to Bundt pan; using a wooden pick, poke holes in bottom of cake. Brush remaining sugar mixture onto bottom of cake. Let stand for 5 minutes. Invert cake onto prepared rack. Carefully remove Bundt pan; let cake cool completely.
9. Place Champagne-Orange Glaze in a large pastry bag fitted with a round piping tip (Wilton No. 10). Carefully pipe glaze into and over grooves of cake, letting excess drip off. Using a large offset spatula, loosen cake from wire rack, and gently transfer to a serving plate. Trace over ridges of cake with glaze, pausing briefly at various points to create a drip effect. Pipe over any bare spots, spreading with a small offset spatula, if needed. Once glaze stops dripping, sprinkle with edible glitter. Garnish with sprinkles, if desired.

CHAMPAGNE-ORANGE GLAZE
Makes about 1 cup

2½ cups (300 grams) confectioners' sugar
¼ cup (56 grams) Champagne or dry sparkling white wine
1 teaspoon (2 grams) tightly packed orange zest
½ teaspoon kosher salt

1. In a medium bowl, stir together all ingredients until smooth and well combined. Use immediately.

CHOCOLATE OLIVE OIL CAKE WITH BLOOD ORANGE GLAZE

Makes 1 (10-cup) Bundt cake

A celebration of citrus season, this chocolate olive oil cake receives a bright boost of color and tang from fresh blood orange juice and zest.

1⅓ cups (276 grams) extra-virgin olive oil
5   large eggs (250 grams), room temperature
1   cup (220 grams) firmly packed light brown sugar
⅔   cup (133 grams) granulated sugar
⅓   cup (80 grams) whole milk, room temperature
2   tablespoons (20 grams) tightly packed blood orange zest
⅓   cup (80 grams) fresh blood orange juice, room temperature
     (from about 5 medium blood oranges)
2   teaspoons (8 grams) vanilla extract
2   cups (250 grams) all-purpose flour
1   cup (85 grams) Dutch process cocoa powder, sifted
2   teaspoons (10 grams) baking powder
2   teaspoons (6 grams) kosher salt
2   teaspoons (4 grams) espresso powder
1   teaspoon (5 grams) baking soda
Blood Orange Glaze (recipe follows)
Garnish: Candied Blood Oranges (recipe follows)

1. Preheat oven to 325°F (170°C).
2. In the bowl of a stand mixer fitted with the whisk attachment, beat oil, eggs, sugars, milk, orange zest and juice, and vanilla at medium-low speed until well combined, 2 to 3 minutes, stopping to scrape sides of bowl.
3. In a medium bowl, whisk together flour, cocoa, baking powder, salt, espresso powder, and baking soda. With mixer on low speed, gradually add flour mixture to oil mixture, beating just until combined and stopping to scrape sides of bowl. (Small lumps in batter are fine; do not overmix.)
4. Spray a 10-cup Bundt pan with baking spray with flour. Spoon batter into prepared pan. Tap pan on a kitchen towel-lined counter

a few times to settle batter and release any air bubbles. (Pan will be quite full, but batter will not overflow during baking.)
5. Bake until a wooden pick inserted near center comes out with just a few moist crumbs, 35 to 45 minutes. Let cool in pan for 20 minutes. Invert cake onto a wire rack placed over a parchment paper-lined rimmed baking sheet; let cool completely.
6. Place Blood Orange Glaze in a pastry bag fitted with a round piping tip (Wilton No. 12). Starting from outside of cake, pipe lines of glaze into grooves. Garnish with Candied Blood Oranges, if desired. Serve with additional Blood Orange Glaze.

BLOOD ORANGE GLAZE

Makes 1 cup

2½   cups (300 grams) confectioners' sugar, sifted
2   tablespoons (28 grams) fresh blood orange juice
     (about 1 medium blood orange)
1½   tablespoons (22.5 grams) whole milk
¼   teaspoon kosher salt

1. In a small bowl, stir together all ingredients until smooth. (Mixture will be very thick.) Use immediately.

CANDIED BLOOD ORANGES

Makes 11 to 13 slices

1   small blood orange (126 grams), cut crosswise into
     ⅛-inch-thick slices
2   cups (400 grams) granulated sugar
2   cups (480 grams) water

1. In a medium saucepan, combine orange slices and cold water to cover by 1 inch. Bring to a boil over medium-high heat. Drain oranges, and repeat procedure once.
2. In a large skillet, bring sugar and 2 cups (480 grams) water to a boil over medium heat and cook, stirring constantly, until sugar dissolves. Add orange slices in a single layer; cook, turning once, until white pith is somewhat translucent and tender, 40 to 45 minutes.
3. Transfer orange slices to a wire rack placed over a baking sheet. Let cool for at least 1 hour or overnight. Reserve syrup for another use.

PRO TIP
For precision, pipe glaze into grooves with a pastry bag fitted with a medium round piping tip.

MARCH

CARROT CHAI BUNDT CAKE

Makes 1 (10-cup) Bundt cake

A surprise swirl of cream cheese filling serves as a nod to classic carrot cake frosting while homemade chai spice adds a subtle zing to the tender cake. A final dusting of Chai Sugar accentuates every ridge and groove, giving this spring cake a well-spiced finish.

3 cups (297 grams) grated peeled carrot
1 cup (220 grams) firmly packed light brown sugar
1 cup (200 grams) granulated sugar, divided
1 cup (214 grams) canola oil
4 large eggs (200 grams), room temperature and divided
1 teaspoon (4 grams) vanilla extract
2 cups (250 grams) plus 1 tablespoon (8 grams) all-purpose flour, divided
2 teaspoons (10 grams) baking soda
1½ teaspoons (3 grams) ground cardamom
1¼ teaspoons (3 grams) kosher salt, divided
1 teaspoon (2 grams) ground cinnamon
¼ teaspoon ground ginger
⅛ teaspoon ground cloves
⅛ teaspoon ground black pepper
½ cup (57 grams) chopped pecans
8 ounces (227 grams) cream cheese, softened (see Note)
Chai Sugar (recipe follows)

1. Preheat oven to 325°F (170°C).
2. In the bowl of a stand mixer fitted with the paddle attachment, beat carrot, brown sugar, ¾ cup (150 grams) granulated sugar, oil, 3 eggs (150 grams), and vanilla at medium-low speed until well combined, 1 to 2 minutes, stopping to scrape sides of bowl.
3. In a medium bowl, whisk together 2 cups (250 grams) flour, baking soda, cardamom, 1 teaspoon (3 grams) salt, cinnamon, ginger, cloves, and pepper. With mixer on low speed, gradually add flour mixture to carrot mixture, beating just until combined and stopping to scrape sides of bowl. Fold in pecans. Transfer to a large bowl.
4. Clean bowl of stand mixer and paddle attachment. Using the paddle attachment, beat cream cheese, remaining ¼ cup (50 grams) granulated sugar, remaining 1 tablespoon (8 grams) flour, and remaining ¼ teaspoon salt at medium speed until smooth, 1 to 2 minutes, stopping to scrape sides of bowl. Add remaining 1 egg (50 grams); beat at medium speed until well combined.

5. Spray a 10-cup Bundt pan with baking spray with flour. Spoon 3 cups batter (about 765 grams) into prepared pan; gently tap pan on counter several times to release air bubbles. Spoon a ring of cream cheese mixture over batter in pan, leaving a ½-inch border around edges of pan. (Cream cheese mixture will have the consistency of cheesecake filling, so you will be able to almost drizzle, rather than dollop, the mixture.) Spoon remaining batter on top, covering cream cheese mixture. Do not tap pan. (Pan will be quite full, but batter will not overflow during baking.)
6. Bake until a wooden pick inserted near center comes out clean, 50 minutes to 1 hour. Let cool in pan for 20 minutes. Invert cake onto a wire rack, and let cool completely. Using a small fine-mesh sieve, dust Chai Sugar onto cooled cake.

Note: *Do not allow cream cheese to get too warm. If overly softened, the filling may sink during baking.*

CHAI SUGAR
Makes 1 cup

1 cup (200 grams) granulated sugar
1 teaspoon (2 grams) ground cinnamon
¾ teaspoon (1.5 grams) ground cardamom
½ teaspoon (1 gram) ground ginger
⅛ teaspoon ground cloves
⅛ teaspoon ground black pepper

1. In the work bowl of a food processor, place all ingredients; process until finely ground, about 5 minutes.

Note: *You will have some Chai Sugar left over. Store in an airtight container for up to 3 months. We love it in our coffee or tea or sprinkled over pound cakes and muffins.*

PRO TIP
For a successful cream cheese swirl, be sure to center your filling within your batter, staying ½ inch away from the sides of the pan.

APRIL

ALMOND BUNDT CAKE WITH COCONUT GLAZE

Makes 1 (6-cup) Bundt cake

Simple, elegant, and a touch whimsical, this Almond Bundt Cake with Coconut Glaze was made with Easter in mind. Using a pan with a 6-cup capacity offers a perfect portion of cake for a cozy family meal. Finish the cake off with toasted coconut to make a centerpiece-worthy cake

¾   cup (170 grams) unsalted butter, softened
1⅓   cups (267 grams) granulated sugar
3   large eggs (150 grams), room temperature
1   teaspoon (4 grams) vanilla extract
½   teaspoon (2 grams) almond extract
1½   cups (187 grams) cake flour
¾   teaspoon (2.25 grams) kosher salt
¼   teaspoon (1.25 grams) baking soda
⅔   cup (160 grams) sour cream, room temperature
Coconut Glaze (recipe follows)
¼   cup (15 grams) toasted sweetened flaked coconut
Garnish: candy-coated chocolate eggs

1. Preheat oven to 325°F (170°C).
2. In the bowl of a stand mixer fitted with the paddle attachment, beat butter and sugar at medium speed until fluffy, 3 to 4 minutes, stopping to scrape sides of bowl. Add eggs, one at a time, beating well after each addition. Beat in extracts.
3. In a medium bowl, whisk together flour, salt, and baking soda. With mixer on low speed, gradually add flour mixture to butter mixture alternately with sour cream, beginning and ending with flour mixture, beating just until combined after each addition. Spoon 1 cup (about 234 grams) batter into a large pastry bag; cut a ¾-inch-wide opening in tip.
4. Spray a 6-cup Bundt pan with baking spray with flour. Using a pastry brush, spread any excess pools of spray in pan and blot brush with a paper towel as needed. Pipe batter directly into grooves of prepared pan to within 2 inches of rim; spoon remaining batter on top. Tap pan on a kitchen towel-lined counter a few times to settle batter and release any air bubbles.

5. Bake until a wooden pick inserted near center comes out with just a few moist crumbs, 40 to 50 minutes. Let cool in pan for 20 minutes. Using a small offset spatula, loosen cake from center of pan. Invert cake onto a wire rack, and let cool completely. Transfer cooled cake to a serving plate.
6. Place Coconut Glaze in a squeezable plastic icing bottle* fitted with a round piping tip (Wilton No. 12). Carefully pipe Coconut Glaze into grooves of cake. Sprinkle flaked coconut on top of cake. Fill center of cake with chocolate eggs, if desired. Serve with extra Coconut Glaze.

We used a 4-ounce Sweet Sugarbelle Icing Bottle with Coupler.

COCONUT GLAZE
Makes ⅔ cup

1   cup (120 grams) confectioners' sugar
3   tablespoons (45 grams) heavy whipping cream
2½   tablespoons (47 grams) cream of coconut

1. In a small bowl, whisk together all ingredients until smooth. Use immediately.

PRO TIP
If you plan on making two of these Bundt cakes in your 6-cup pan, make sure to prepare your second batch of batter after the first cake has been baked off and removed from the Bundt pan. Doubling the batter will mean that one half will sit out while the other cake bakes, affecting the second cake's texture. It's best to make one batter, bake it off, and then make the second batter after your Bundt pan has been cooled and cleaned.

CHURRO BUNDT CAKE

Makes 1 (10-cup) Bundt cake

Packed with sugar and spice, this warm vanilla Bundt is a churro in cake form. The cinnamon filling and crunchy cinnamon-sugar coating act as a nod to the Spanish street food's crispy exterior. For an extra kick of sweet heat, drizzle each slice with our indulgent Mexican Chocolate Sauce.

¾   cup (170 grams) unsalted butter, softened
1½   cups (300 grams) granulated sugar, divided
¾   cup (165 grams) plus 2 tablespoons (28 grams) firmly packed
     light brown sugar, divided
4   large eggs (200 grams), room temperature
1   large egg yolk (19 grams), room temperature
2½   teaspoons (10 grams) vanilla extract
2¾   cups (344 grams) cake flour
2   teaspoons (10 grams) baking powder
¾   teaspoon (2.25 grams) kosher salt
½   teaspoon (2.5 grams) baking soda
1¼   cups (290 grams) full-fat Greek yogurt,
     room temperature
⅓   cup (80 grams) whole milk, room temperature
2½   teaspoons (5 grams) ground cinnamon, divided
2   tablespoons (28 grams) unsalted butter, melted
Mexican Chocolate Sauce (recipe follows)

1. Preheat oven to 350°F (180°C).
2. In the bowl of a stand mixer fitted with the paddle attachment, beat softened butter, 1¼ cups (250 grams) granulated sugar, and ¼ cup (55 grams) brown sugar at medium speed until fluffy, 3 to 4 minutes, stopping to scrape sides of bowl. Add eggs and egg yolk, one at a time, beating well after each addition. Beat in vanilla. (Mixture may look slightly curdled at this point, but batter will come together.)
3. In a medium bowl, whisk together flour, baking powder, salt, and baking soda. In a small bowl, whisk together yogurt and milk. With mixer on low speed, gradually add flour mixture to butter mixture alternately with yogurt mixture, beginning and ending with flour mixture, beating just until combined after each addition. (Batter will be thick.)

4. In a small bowl, stir together ½ cup (110 grams) brown sugar and 1½ teaspoons (3 grams) cinnamon. Set aside.
5. Spray a 10-cup Bundt pan with baking spray with flour. Using a pastry brush, spread any excess spray in pan, blotting brush with a paper towel as needed. (This helps to better fill the pan's grooves with batter, resulting in a sharper design after baking.) Spoon one-fourth of batter (1¼ cups [about 345 grams]) into prepared pan. Tap pan on a kitchen towel-lined counter a few times to settle batter and release any air bubbles. Spoon one-fourth of batter into pan, and tap pan on counter. Spoon brown sugar mixture in a ring onto batter in pan, leaving a ¼-inch border around edges of pan. (Brown sugar layer will be thick.) Spoon remaining batter onto brown sugar mixture. Using a small offset spatula, smooth top, pushing batter into sides of pan.
6. Bake until a wooden pick inserted near center comes out clean, 50 to 55 minutes. Let cool in pan for 10 minutes. Using a small offset spatula, loosen cake from center of pan. Invert pan onto a wire rack placed over a rimmed baking sheet; let cake cool in pan for 10 minutes. Remove pan, and let cake cool completely.
7. In a small bowl, stir together remaining ¼ cup (50 grams) granulated sugar, remaining 2 tablespoons (28 grams) brown sugar, and remaining 1 teaspoon (2 grams) cinnamon. Brush cake with melted butter, and cover with granulated sugar mixture, pressing gently to adhere. Serve with Mexican Chocolate Sauce.

Mexican Chocolate Sauce
Makes about 1 cup

⅓   cup (80 grams) heavy whipping cream
¼   cup (57 grams) unsalted butter
½   cup (100 grams) granulated sugar
⅓   cup (25 grams) unsweetened cocoa powder, sifted
3   tablespoons (63 grams) light corn syrup
½   teaspoon (1 gram) ground cinnamon
¼   teaspoon kosher salt
⅛   teaspoon ground red pepper
0.5 ounce (14 grams) unsweetened chocolate
2   teaspoons (10 grams) coffee liqueur

1. In a medium saucepan, heat cream and butter over medium-low heat until butter is melted. Add sugar; cook, whisking frequently, until sugar is mostly dissolved, 6 to 8 minutes. Add cocoa, corn syrup, cinnamon, salt, and red pepper; cook, whisking constantly, until smooth and well combined, 2 to 3 minutes. Stir in chocolate until melted. Remove from heat; stir in liqueur. Serve warm. Refrigerate leftovers. To reheat, microwave on high in 10-second intervals, stirring between each, until melted and smooth.

KEY LIME BUNDT CAKE

Makes 1 (10-cup) Bundt cake

Packed with lime zest and soaked in lime juice, this bright Key Lime Bundt Cake offers all the zing and freshness of a Key lime pie. Sprinkled with graham cracker crumbs as a nod to the original pie's buttery crumb crust, this cake is summer by the slice.

1¾   cups (350 grams) granulated sugar, divided
½   cup (110 grams) firmly packed light brown sugar
3   tablespoons (10 grams) packed Key lime zest
     (about 3 medium limes)
1   cup (227 grams) unsalted butter, softened
4   large eggs (200 grams), room temperature
3   cups (375 grams) cake flour
1   teaspoon (3 grams) kosher salt
½   teaspoon (2.5 grams) baking soda
1¼   cups (300 grams) whole buttermilk, room temperature
1   tablespoon (14 grams) all-vegetable shortening, melted
½   cup (62 grams) dry plain bread crumbs
⅓   cup (80 grams) Key lime juice (from bottle)
Buttermilk Glaze (recipe follows)
Garnish: finely ground graham cracker crumbs, lime zest

1. Preheat oven to 325°F (170°C).
2. In a medium bowl, stir together 1½ cups (300 grams) granulated sugar, brown sugar, and lime zest until well combined.
3. In the bowl of a stand mixer fitted with the paddle attachment, beat sugar mixture and butter at medium speed until fluffy, 3 to 4 minutes, stopping to scrape sides of bowl. Add eggs, one at a time, beating well after each addition. (Mixture may look curdled at this point, but batter will come together.)

4. In a medium bowl, whisk together flour, salt, and baking soda. With mixer on low speed, gradually add flour mixture to sugar mixture alternately with buttermilk, beginning and ending with flour mixture, beating just until combined after each addition and stopping to scrape sides of bowl.
5. Using a small pastry brush, thoroughly grease a 10-cup Bundt pan with melted shortening. Coat inside of pan with bread crumbs, shaking out excess. Spoon batter into prepared pan. Tap pan on a kitchen towel-lined counter a few times to settle batter and release any air bubbles. (Pan will be quite full, but batter will not overflow during baking.)
6. Bake until a wooden pick inserted near center comes out clean, 50 minutes to 1 hour. Let cool in pan for 10 minutes. Using a small offset spatula, gently loosen cake from center of pan. Invert pan onto a wire rack placed over a parchment paper-lined rimmed baking sheet; let cake cool in pan for 10 minutes. Remove pan.
7. In a small bowl, stir together lime juice and remaining ¼ cup (50 grams) granulated sugar. Gently brush juice mixture all over cake. Let cool completely.
8. Using a large spoon, spoon Buttermilk Glaze all over cake. To coat sides, drizzle additional Buttermilk Glaze, and spread with back of spoon. Garnish with graham cracker crumbs and lime zest, if desired.

BUTTERMILK GLAZE

Makes about 1⅓ cups

3   cups (360 grams) confectioners' sugar
⅓   cup (80 grams) whole buttermilk
2½   tablespoons (52.5 grams) light corn syrup
1¼   teaspoons (5 grams) vanilla extract
½   teaspoon (1.5 grams) kosher salt

1. In a large bowl, stir together all ingredients until smooth. Use immediately.

PRO TIP
Glaze this cake on a wire rack placed over a parchment-lined baking sheet, allowing any excess to drip off. This way, extra glaze can be scooped up and served alongside this beautiful Bundt. Plus, the parchment makes for easier cleanup.

JULY

Makes 1 (10-cup) Bundt cake

Packed with red and blue sprinkles and filled with raspberry sorbet, this tender lemon-scented Bundt cake has all-American flair in every slice. Garnished with a creamy patriotic-hued glaze and star-spangled sprinkles, this dazzling Bundt is the sweetest way to celebrate the Fourth of July.

1⅔ cups (333 grams) granulated sugar
3 tablespoons (9 grams) lemon zest (about 4 medium lemons)
3 large eggs (150 grams), room temperature
1 teaspoon (4 grams) vanilla extract
2½ cups (312 grams) cake flour
2 teaspoons (10 grams) baking powder
1 teaspoon (3 grams) kosher salt
⅔ cup (149 grams) canola oil
½ cup (120 grams) whole milk, room temperature
¼ cup (46 grams) red sprinkles
¼ cup (46 grams) blue sprinkles
1 (16-ounce) container (455 grams) raspberry sorbet, slightly softened
Vanilla Glaze (recipe follows)
Garnish: assorted sprinkles

1. Preheat oven to 325°F (170°C).
2. In the bowl of a stand mixer fitted with the paddle attachment, beat sugar and lemon zest at medium speed until fragrant and well combined, 1 to 2 minutes, stopping to scrape sides of bowl. Add eggs and vanilla, and beat until light yellow, slightly thickened, and well combined, 1 to 2 minutes.
3. In a medium bowl, whisk together flour, baking powder, and salt. In a small bowl, whisk together oil and milk. With mixer on low speed, gradually add flour mixture to sugar mixture alternately with oil mixture, beginning and ending with flour mixture, beating until well combined after each addition and stopping to scrape sides of bowl. Fold in sprinkles.
4. Spray a 10-cup Bundt pan with baking spray with flour. Spoon batter into prepared pan. Tap pan on a kitchen towel–lined counter a few times to settle batter and release any air bubbles.
5. Bake until a wooden pick inserted near center comes out with just a few moist crumbs, 40 to 45 minutes. Let cool in pan for 10 minutes. Using a small offset spatula, gently loosen cake from

PATRIOTIC SPRINKLE CAKE

center of pan. Invert cake onto a wire rack, and let cool slightly, about 1 hour.
6. Turn cake upside down. Using a small serrated knife, cut a 1½-inch-wide channel in bottom of cake, leaving a ¾-inch border around edges of pan. Using a small spoon, remove top layer (¼ to ½ inch thick) from channel, keeping large pieces intact; set aside. Continue to hollow out a 1½-inch-deep tunnel, reserving removed cake pieces. Freeze hollowed cake for 30 minutes.
7. Spoon sorbet into tunnel; cover with reserved top cake layer. Use additional removed cake pieces to seal any holes. (Reserve remaining cake crumbs for another use.) Cover and freeze cake upside down for at least 4 hours or overnight.
8. Remove cake from freezer and turn right side up. Place Vanilla Glaze in pastry bags fitted with fitted with round piping tips (Wilton No. 10). Starting from outside of cake, pipe lines of Vanilla Glaze into grooves. Garnish with sprinkles, if desired. Let stand at room temperature for 15 minutes. Serve with extra Vanilla Glaze.

Vanilla Glaze
Makes about 1½ cups

3¼ cups (390 grams) confectioners' sugar
¼ cup (60 grams) whole milk
2 tablespoons (28 grams) unsalted butter, melted
1 teaspoon (4 grams) vanilla extract
½ teaspoon (1.5 grams) kosher salt
22 drops red food coloring
10 drops blue food coloring

1. In a large bowl, stir together confectioners' sugar, milk, melted butter, vanilla, and salt until smooth. Divide glaze among 3 bowls (about ½ cup [146 grams] each). Add red food coloring to first bowl, stirring to combine. Add blue food coloring to second bowl, stirring to combine. Leave remaining bowl plain. Use immediately.

PRO TIP
Using a ¼-cup spring-loaded scoop makes adding this thinner cake batter to the pan clean and simple.

AUGUST

S'MORES SWIRL BUNDT CAKE

Makes 1 (6-cup) Bundt cake

Make all of your s'mores dreams come true, no campfire needed. This cake features two piped cake batters—graham cracker and black cocoa—that make a mesmerizing spiral and is finished off with an indulgent Milk Chocolate Ganache that echoes the melted interior of your favorite campfire snack. A topper of toasted marshmallows, crushed graham crackers, and milk chocolate chunks makes for a photogenic finish.

¾   cup (170 grams) unsalted butter, softened
1⅓ cups (267 grams) granulated sugar
3   large eggs (150 grams), room temperature
1   tablespoon (13 grams) vanilla extract
1   cup plus 2 tablespoons (141 grams) cake flour
⅔   cup (75 grams) finely ground graham cracker
    crumbs (5 to 6 crackers)
¾   teaspoon (2.25 grams) kosher salt
¼   teaspoon (1.25 grams) baking soda
½   cup (120 grams) whole buttermilk, room temperature
2   tablespoons (10 grams) black cocoa powder
¼   teaspoon espresso powder
Milk Chocolate Ganache (recipe follows)
Large marshmallows
Garnish: broken milk chocolate bars, roughly crushed graham
    crackers

1. Preheat oven to 325°F (170°C). Spray a 6-cup Bundt pan with baking spray with flour. Using a pastry brush, spread any excess spray in pan, blotting brush with a paper towel as needed. Freeze pan for 20 minutes. (See Note.)
2. In the bowl of a stand mixer fitted with the paddle attachment, beat butter and sugar at medium speed until fluffy, 3 to 4 minutes, stopping to scrape sides of bowl. Add eggs, one at a time, beating well after each addition. Beat in vanilla. (Mixture may look slightly curdled at this point, but batter will come together.)
3. In a medium bowl, whisk together flour, graham cracker crumbs, salt, and baking soda. With mixer on low speed, gradually add flour mixture to butter mixture alternately with buttermilk, beginning and ending with flour mixture, beating just until combined after each addition.
4. In a small bowl, whisk together black cocoa and espresso powder. Transfer about 2 cups (about 458 grams) batter to a medium bowl; fold in black cocoa mixture until well combined.

5. Spoon 1 cup (about 228 grams) black cocoa batter into a large pastry bag. Spoon 1 cup (about 228 grams) plain batter into another large pastry bag. Cut a ¼-inch opening in tip of each bag. Alternately pipe batters directly into grooves of prepared pan to within ¾ inch from top of outside rim and top of center tube, being careful not to spill into neighboring grooves. Using a small offset spatula or a wooden pick, carefully spread batter into grooves and up sides of pan. Continue to pipe and spread more batter into each groove, using offset spatula or wooden pick to close any gaps between batters. (Be sure to wipe off spatula or wooden pick as needed to avoid smearing colors.) Refill pastry bags with remaining batters; pipe into pan, continuing to follow pattern. Tap pan on counter several times to spread batter into grooves and release any air bubbles.
6. Bake until a wooden pick inserted near center comes out clean, 45 to 50 minutes. Let cool in pan for 10 minutes. Using a small offset spatula, loosen cake from center of pan. Invert cake onto a wire rack, and let cool completely. Transfer cooled cake to a serving plate.
7. Place Milk Chocolate Ganache in a 4-ounce squeezable plastic icing bottle fitted with a round piping tip (Wilton No. 10.) Carefully pipe Milk Chocolate Ganache into grooves of cooled cake. Fill center of cake with marshmallows. Using a handheld kitchen torch, carefully and lightly toast marshmallows. Garnish with chocolate and graham crackers, if desired. Serve with extra Milk Chocolate Ganache.

Note: *Freezing the pan helps the batter cling to the sides of the pan while being precisely piped and spread.*

MILK CHOCOLATE GANACHE
Makes about ¾ cup

6   ounces (175 grams) milk chocolate candy bars, chopped
⅓   cup (80 grams) heavy whipping cream

1. In a small heatproof bowl, place chocolate.
2. In a small saucepan, heat cream over medium-low heat just until bubbles form around edges of pan. (Do not boil.) Pour hot cream over chocolate. Let stand for 2 minutes; stir until chocolate is melted and mixture is smooth. Use immediately.

APPLE PECAN SPICE CAKE WITH TOFFEE GLAZE

SEPTEMBER

Makes 1 (10-cup) Bundt cake

Serve up a slice of fall comfort with this soul-warming Apple Pecan Spice Cake with Toffee Glaze. Studded with tart Honeycrisp apples and buttery pecans, this tender cake makes the most of the season's harvest. An indulgent Toffee Glaze gives this recipe the candied flavor and glistening exterior of a caramel apple.

1¾ cups (385 grams) firmly packed dark brown sugar
1   cup (224 grams) canola oil
¾   cup (180 grams) sour cream, room temperature
3   large eggs (150 grams), room temperature
1   tablespoon (13 grams) vanilla extract
3   cups (375 grams) all-purpose flour
1   teaspoon (5 grams) baking soda
1   teaspoon (3 grams) kosher salt
1   teaspoon (2 grams) ground allspice
1   teaspoon (2 grams) ground cinnamon
¾   teaspoon (1.5 grams) ground nutmeg
¼   teaspoon ground cloves
2   cups (250 grams) ¼-inch-diced peeled Honeycrisp apples
     (about 2 large apples)
¾   cup (85 grams) roughly chopped toasted pecans
Toffee Glaze (recipe follows)
Garnish: chopped toasted pecans, flaked sea salt

1. Preheat oven to 325°F (170°C).
2. In the bowl of a stand mixer fitted with the paddle attachment, beat brown sugar, oil, sour cream, eggs, and vanilla at medium speed until well combined, 1 to 2 minutes.
3. In a medium bowl, whisk together flour, baking soda, kosher salt, allspice, cinnamon, nutmeg, and cloves. With mixer on low speed, gradually add flour mixture to sugar mixture, beating just until combined. Fold in apples and pecans. (Batter will be thick and it may seem like you have too many apples, but it will be fine.)

4. Spray a 10-cup Bundt pan with baking spray with flour. Using a pastry brush, spread any excess spray in pan, blotting brush with a paper towel as needed. Using a ¼-cup spring-loaded scoop, scoop batter into prepared pan. Tap pan on a kitchen towel-lined counter a few times to settle batter and release any air bubbles. (Pan will be quite full, but batter will not overflow during baking.)
5. Bake until a wooden pick inserted near center comes out with a few moist crumbs, 1 hour and 5 minutes to 1 hour and 15 minutes. Let cool in pan for 10 minutes. Using a small offset spatula, gently loosen cake from center of pan. Invert pan onto a wire rack placed over a rimmed baking sheet, and let cake cool in pan for 10 minutes. Remove pan, and let cake cool completely.
6. Spoon Toffee Glaze all over cooled cake. Drizzle glaze onto sides, and spread with the back of a spoon. Garnish with pecans and sea salt, if desired. Let stand for 15 minutes; transfer cake to a serving plate. Serve with any extra Toffee Glaze.

TOFFEE GLAZE
Makes 1⅔ cups

1   cup (220 grams) firmly packed dark brown sugar
⅔   cup (226 grams) dark corn syrup
⅓   cup (80 grams) heavy whipping cream
¼   cup (57 grams) unsalted butter, cubed
¼   teaspoon kosher salt
½   teaspoon (2 grams) vanilla extract

1. In a medium saucepan, bring brown sugar, corn syrup, cream, butter, and salt to a boil over medium-high heat; cook, whisking constantly, for 2 minutes. Remove from heat; whisk in vanilla. Transfer mixture to a medium heatproof bowl. Let cool for 20 minutes. Use immediately.

PRO TIP
If the Toffee Glaze begins to set up, microwave on high in 10-second intervals, stirring between each, until melted and smooth.

PUMPKIN MASCARPONE BUNDT CAKE WITH MASCARPONE GLAZE

OCTOBER

Makes 1 (10-cup) Bundt cake

For heightened decadence and complexity, this cake paired the ultimate flavor of fall, pumpkin, with mascarpone, folding it into this cake's batter and using it as the base for the glaze. Mascarpone's slight tang enhances the buttery, subtly sweet taste of pumpkin—along with vanilla, orange zest, and soul-warming pumpkin pie spice. The pumpkin-mascarpone combo also creates an ultra-moist, delightfully dense, and creamy texture.

1¼ cups (250 grams) granulated sugar
¼ cup (55 grams) firmly packed light brown sugar
3 large eggs (150 grams), room temperature
1 (15-ounce) can (425 grams) pumpkin
8 ounces (226 grams) mascarpone cheese, softened
⅓ cup (76 grams) unsalted butter, melted and cooled
2 teaspoons (8 grams) vanilla extract
1 teaspoon (3 grams) tightly packed orange zest
2¼ cups (281 grams) unbleached cake flour
2½ teaspoons (5 grams) pumpkin pie spice
1½ teaspoons (7.5 grams) baking powder
1 teaspoon (3 grams) kosher salt
¾ teaspoon (3.75 grams) baking soda
1 tablespoon (14 grams) all-vegetable shortening, melted
Mascarpone Glaze (recipe follows)
Garnish: pumpkin pie spice, pepitas

1. Preheat oven to 350°F (180°C).
2. In the bowl of a stand mixer fitted with the paddle attachment, beat sugars and eggs at medium speed until fluffy and light in color, 2 to 3 minutes. Add pumpkin, mascarpone, melted butter, vanilla, and orange zest; beat at medium-low speed until well combined, 1 to 2 minutes, stopping to scrape sides of bowl. (Mixture may look curdled at this point, but batter will come together.)

3. In a large bowl, whisk together flour, pie spice, baking powder, salt, and baking soda. With mixer on low speed, gradually add flour mixture to sugar mixture, beating just until combined.
4. Using a small pastry brush, coat inside of a 10-cup Bundt pan with melted shortening. Spoon batter into prepared pan. Tap pan on a kitchen towel-lined counter a few times to settle batter and release any air bubbles. (Pan will be quite full, but batter will not overflow during baking.)
5. Bake until a wooden pick inserted near center comes out clean, 55 to 58 minutes. Let cool in pan for 10 minutes. Using a small offset spatula, gently loosen cake from center of pan. Invert cake onto a wire rack placed over a parchment-lined baking sheet, and let cool completely.
6. Working quickly, spoon Mascarpone Glaze over top of cake. Drizzle glaze onto and between outer ridges, spreading with the back of a spoon or a small offset spatula to cover completely. (Scoop and reuse excess glaze pooled on parchment paper, if necessary.) Garnish with pie spice and pepitas, if desired.

MASCARPONE GLAZE
Makes about 1½ cups

3½ cups (420 grams) confectioners' sugar, sifted
5 tablespoons (75 grams) whole milk
¼ cup (52 grams) mascarpone cheese, softened
½ teaspoon (1.5 grams) kosher salt

1. In a medium bowl, stir together all ingredients until smooth. Use immediately.

PRO TIP
A coat of melted shortening ensures this tight-crumbed Bundt's batter bakes beautifully into and releases cleanly from the pan. When coating the pan, use a small pastry brush to make sure the shortening gets into every narrow, angular groove.

NOVEMBER

PECAN PIE BUNDT CAKE

Makes 1 (10-cup) Bundt cake

This cake brings you fall's favorite pie now in Bundt cake form. Toasted pecans give texture and signature pecan pie flavor to this buttery cake, and a splash of bourbon makes for an extra-tender crumb. Coat the Bundt pan in finely chopped pecans to create an eye-catching (and irresistibly crunchy) design on the outside of the cake. Top it off with a boozy Brown Sugar-Bourbon Sauce for a memorable dessert that'll be the star of your harvest table.

1½	cups (340 grams) unsalted butter, softened
2	cups (400 grams) granulated sugar
¼	cup (55 grams) firmly packed light brown sugar
3	large eggs (150 grams), room temperature
1	teaspoon (4 grams) vanilla extract
3	cups (375 grams) all-purpose flour
1¼	teaspoons (3.75 grams) kosher salt
¼	teaspoon (1.25 grams) baking soda
1	cup (240 grams) heavy whipping cream, room temperature
2	teaspoons (10 grams) bourbon
½	cup (57 grams) finely chopped toasted pecans
½	cup (57 grams) super finely chopped raw pecans

Toasted pecan halves (optional)
Brown Sugar-Bourbon Sauce (recipe follows)

1. Preheat oven to 325°F (170°C).
2. In the bowl of a stand mixer fitted with the paddle attachment, beat butter and sugars at medium speed until fluffy, 3 to 4 minutes, stopping to scrape sides of bowl. Add eggs, one at a time, beating well after each addition; scrape sides of bowl. Beat in vanilla.
3. In a medium bowl, whisk together flour, salt, and baking soda. In a small bowl, whisk together cream and bourbon. Add flour mixture to butter mixture alternately with cream mixture, beginning and ending with flour mixture, beating just until combined after each addition and stopping to scrape sides of bowl. Fold in chopped toasted pecans.

4. Spray a 10-cup Bundt pan with baking spray with flour. Coat inside of pan with raw pecans, turning to coat and shaking out any excess. Spoon batter into prepared pan. Tap pan on a kitchen towel-lined counter a few times to settle batter and release any air bubbles. (Pan will be quite full, but batter will not overflow during baking.)
5. Bake until a wooden pick inserted near center comes out clean, 1 hour to 1 hour and 15 minutes. Let cool in pan for 15 minutes. Using a small offset spatula, gently loosen center and edges of cake from pan. Invert pan onto a wire rack; let cake cool in pan for 20 minutes. Pick up wire rack with Bundt pan on top, and lightly tap on counter to loosen cake; remove pan, and place wire rack over a parchment-lined baking sheet. Let cake cool completely.
6. Top each petal of cake design with 1 pecan half (if using). Spoon Brown Sugar-Bourbon Sauce over ridges of cake as desired. Once sauce stops dripping, transfer cake to a serving plate. For fuller coverage, quickly brush more still-hot sauce onto sides of cake using a small pastry brush. Serve immediately.

BROWN SUGAR-BOURBON SAUCE
Makes about 1⅓ cups

1	cup (220 grams) firmly packed light brown sugar
½	cup (113 grams) unsalted butter
¼	cup (60 grams) heavy whipping cream
¼	teaspoon kosher salt
1	teaspoon (5 grams) bourbon

1. In a small saucepan, bring brown sugar, butter, cream, and salt to a boil over medium heat. Remove from heat; stir in bourbon. Use immediately.

PRO TIP
Coating the pan with baking spray with flour and finely chopped raw pecans gives the final cake a smooth exterior and a toasted, nutty finish.

RED VELVET BUNDT CAKE

DECEMBER

Makes 1 (10-cup) Bundt cake

We reimagined everyone's favorite holiday layer cake as a red velvet cake brimming with cheer. You'll come for the tender red velvet cake and stay for the vanilla bean seed-speckled Cream Cheese Filling that echoes the original's cream cheese frosting. For an even more festive look, garnish your cake plate or cake stand with branches of sugared rosemary.

1¼	cups (284 grams) unsalted butter, softened
2	cups (400 grams) granulated sugar
3	large eggs (150 grams), room temperature
1	large egg yolk (19 grams), room temperature
1½	teaspoons (6 grams) vanilla extract
2	cups (250 grams) all-purpose flour
½	cup (43 grams) unsweetened cocoa powder
1½	teaspoons (7.5 grams) baking powder
¾	teaspoon (2.25 grams) kosher salt
1	cup (240 grams) whole buttermilk
1	(1-ounce) bottle (29 grams) liquid red food coloring

Cream Cheese Filling (recipe follows)
Garnish: confectioners' sugar, sugared rosemary

1. Preheat oven to 350°F (180°C).

2. In the bowl of a stand mixer fitted with the paddle attachment, beat butter and granulated sugar at medium speed until fluffy, 3 to 4 minutes, stopping to scrape sides of bowl. Add eggs and egg yolk, one at a time, beating well after each addition. Beat in vanilla.

3. In a medium bowl, whisk together flour, cocoa, baking powder, and salt. Gradually add flour mixture to butter mixture alternately with buttermilk, beginning and ending with flour mixture, beating just until combined after each addition and stopping to scrape sides of bowl. Add food coloring, and stir until combined.

4. Spray a 10-cup Bundt pan with baking spray with flour. Spoon two-thirds of batter (about 936 grams) into prepared pan. Gently tap pan on counter several times. Using a small spoon, make a well in center of batter, slightly pushing batter up sides and center of pan. Spoon Cream Cheese Filling into well, making sure filling does not touch sides of pan, and gently tap on counter to release any air bubbles. Using a knife, swirl filling and batter, being careful not to touch sides of pan. Spoon remaining batter on top. Swirl filling and batter again, being careful not to touch sides of pan. Tap pan on a kitchen towel-lined counter a few times to settle batter and release any air bubbles. Smooth top with an offset spatula.

5. Bake until a wooden pick inserted near center comes out clean, 1 hour and 5 minutes to 1 hour and 10 minutes. Remove from oven, and immediately tap pan on counter 4 to 5 times to release any air bubbles from Cream Cheese Filling. Let cool in pan for 30 minutes. Invert pan onto a wire rack, and let cake cool in pan for 5 minutes. Remove pan, and let cake cool completely. Garnish with confectioners' sugar and sugared rosemary, if desired. Cover and refrigerate for up to 3 days.

CREAM CHEESE FILLING

Makes about 1⅓ cups

8	ounces (226 grams) cream cheese, softened
1	tablespoon (14 grams) unsalted butter, softened
½	cup (60 grams) confectioners' sugar
1	large egg yolk (19 grams)
½	teaspoon (2 grams) vanilla extract

1. In a medium bowl, beat cream cheese and butter with a mixer at medium speed until combined and smooth, about 2 minutes. Add confectioners' sugar, egg yolk, and vanilla. Beat until smooth, about 1 minute.

PRO TIP
If the filling touches the pan, it allows the cake to crack easily, and the cake will split when removed from the pan. Creating a well for the filling in the center of the batter helps keep the filling from the edges.

recipe index

CHOCOLATE

Black-and-White Chocolate Marble Pound Cake 43
Black Cocoa Bundt Cake 47
Chocolate-Carrot Bundt Cake 32
Chocolate Chip Kugelhopf 36
Chocolate-Coconut Bundt Cake 39
Chocolate Olive Oil Cake with Blood Orange Glaze 174
Chocolate Pound Cake with Hot Fudge Sauce 130
Double-Chocolate Spice Bundt Cake 44
German Chocolate Cake with Butterscotch Glaze 48
Mexican Hot Chocolate Bundt Cake 31
Peanut Butter and Chocolate Swirl Bundt Cake 35
Peppermint Swirl Pound Cake 118
Red Velvet Bundt Cake 194
Rocky Road Bundt Cake 50
S'mores Swirl Bundt Cake 187

CREAM CHEESE

Banana Bundt Cake with Cream Cheese Swirl 115
Carrot Chai Bundt Cake 177
Chai Butternut Squash Bundt Cake 156
Chocolate-Carrot Bundt Cake 32
Cinnamon Swirl Bundt Cake 111
Hummingbird Bundt Cake 88
In-Flight Bundt Cake 109
Italian Cream Bundt Cake 145
Peach Pound Cake 106
Peppermint Swirl Pound Cake 118
Red Velvet Bundt Cake 194
Roasted Banana Rum Bundt Cake 63
Strawberry Swirl Pound Cake 112
Ultimate Cream Cheese-Vanilla Bean Pound Cake 142

FROSTINGS, FILLINGS, GARNISHES, AND GLAZES

Basque Custard 129
Bittersweet Chocolate Glaze 44
Black Cocoa Glaze 43
Blood Orange Glaze 174
Bourbon Caramel Sauce 72
Bourbon-Vanilla Caramel Sauce 54
Brown Sugar-Bourbon Sauce 193
Buttermilk Glaze 96, 106, 168, 182
Buttermilk Orange Glaze 112
Butterscotch Glaze 48
Cane Syrup Glaze 94
Champagne-Orange Glaze 173
Chocolate Glaze 31
Citrus Glaze 84
Coconut Glaze 179
Cookie Butter Glaze 109
Cream Cheese Filling 194
Cream Cheese Glaze 32, 111, 118
Cream Cheese Icing 88
Crème Fraîche Glaze 83
Dark Rum Glaze 60

Hot Fudge Sauce 130
Kahlúa Glaze 57
Kahlúa Pecan Filling 57
Lemon Glaze 101
Marshmallow Glaze 50
Mascarpone Glaze 190
Mexican Chocolate Sauce 180
Milk Chocolate Ganache 187
Peanut Butter Frosting 35
Rum Glaze 68
Satsuma Glaze 102
Spiced Rum Glaze 67
Spiced Streusel 84
Spiced Vanilla Chantilly Crème 65
Toasted Sesame Frosting 125
Toffee Glaze 188
Vanilla Almond Glaze 147
Vanilla Bean-Brandy Glaze 76
Vanilla Bean Glaze 43, 47
Vanilla Cream Cheese Glaze 63
Vanilla Glaze 185
Vanilla Rum Syrup 65
Walnut Syrup 156

FRUIT

APPLE
Apple Butter Bundt Cake 86
Apple-Cinnamon Sugar Doughnut Bundt Cake 161
Apple Pecan Spice Cake with Toffee Glaze 188
Candied Apple & Pear Bundt Cake 94

BANANA
Banana Bundt Cake with Cream Cheese Swirl 115
Hummingbird Bundt Cake 88
Roasted Banana Rum Bundt Cake 63

BERRIES
Almond-Strawberry Bundt Cake 80
Brown Sugar Bundt Cake with Bourbon Cherries 59
Butter Cake with Browned Butter Strawberry Syrup 99
Cherries Jubilee Bundt Cake 76
Cranberry Streusel Bundt Cake 84
Lemon-Blueberry Buttermilk Pound Cake 96
Patriotic Sprinkle Cake 185
Peanut Butter and Jelly Swirl Bundt Cake 116
Strawberry Swirl Pound Cake 112

CITRUS
Chocolate Olive Oil Cake with Blood Orange Glaze 174
Key Lime Bundt Cake 182
Lemon-Blueberry Buttermilk Pound Cake 96
Lemon Poppy Seed Bundt Cake 101
Lemon Pound Cake 126
Orange-Sour Cream Pound Cake 93
Patriotic Sprinkle Cake 185
Satsuma-Vanilla Bundt Cake 102

COCONUT
Almond Bundt Cake with Coconut Glaze 179
Chocolate-Coconut Bundt Cake 39
Coconut Bundt Cake 132

Italian Cream Bundt Cake 145
Spiced Coconut Oil Cake with Bourbon Glaze 162

STONE FRUIT
Peach and Cardamom Bundt Cake 83
Peach Pound Cake 106

MISCELLANEOUS

Bourbon Cherries 59
Candied Blood Oranges 174
Candied Orange Rind 36
Chai Sugar 177
Cranberry Powder 84
Roasted Bananas 63
Sugared Spice Blend 151

NUTS

ALMOND
Almond Bundt Cake with Coconut Glaze 179
Almond Poppy Seed Bundt Cake 137
Almond Pound Cake 126
Almond-Strawberry Bundt Cake 80
Birthday Cake Bundt 147
Original German Pound Cake 22
Rocky Road Bundt Cake 50

PEANUT, PISTACHIO & WALNUT
Chai Butternut Squash Bundt Cake 156
Peanut Butter and Jelly Swirl Bundt Cake 116
Peanut Butter and Chocolate Swirl Bundt Cake 35
Snickerdoodle Swirl Bundt Cake with Salted Pistachios 165

PECAN
Apple Pecan Spice Cake with Toffee Glaze 188
Brown Sugar-Bourbon Pound Cake 72
Carrot Chai Bundt Cake 177
Fruitcake Bundt 71
Hummingbird Bundt Cake 88
Italian Cream Bundt Cake 145
Pecan Pie Bundt Cake 193
Spiced Coconut Oil Cake with Bourbon Glaze 162
Spiced Sweet Potato Bundt Cake 155

SPICE

Apple Butter Bundt Cake 86
Apple-Cinnamon Sugar Doughnut Bundt Cake 161
Apple Pecan Spice Cake with Toffee Glaze 188
Banana Bundt Cake with Cream Cheese Swirl 115
Brown Sugar Bundt Cake with Toasted Sesame Frosting 125
Butter Cake with Browned Butter Strawberry Syrup 99
Candied Apple & Pear Bundt Cake 94
Carrot Chai Bundt Cake 177
Chai Butternut Squash Bundt Cake 156
Chocolate-Carrot Bundt Cake 32
Churro Bundt Cake 180
Cinnamon Swirl Bundt Cake 111

Cranberry Streusel Bundt Cake 84
Double-Chocolate Spice Bundt Cake 44
Easy Spiced Swirl Bundt Cake 151
Eggnog Bundt Cake 68
Fruitcake Bundt 71
Gingerbread Bundt Cake with Buttermilk Glaze 168
Hummingbird Bundt Cake 88
Mexican Hot Chocolate Bundt Cake 31
Pain d'Épice 152
Peach and Cardamom Bundt Cake 83
Pumpkin Mascarpone Bundt Cake with Mascarpone Glaze 190
Rum Raisin Bundt Cake 67
Snickerdoodle Swirl Bundt Cake with Salted Pistachios 165
Spiced Bundt Cake 167
Spiced Coconut Oil Cake with Bourbon Glaze 162
Spiced Sweet Potato Bundt Cake 155

WINE & SPIRITS

BOURBON/WHISKEY
Banana Bundt Cake with Cream Cheese Swirl 115
Beaumes-de-Venise Bundt Cake with Apricots 75
Brown Sugar-Bourbon Pound Cake 72
Brown Sugar Bundt Cake with Bourbon Cherries 59
Cherries Jubilee Bundt Cake 76
Dark 'n Stormy Bundt Cake 60
Eggnog Bundt Cake 68
Fruitcake Bundt 71
Mimosa Bundt Cake 173
Pecan Pie Bundt Cake 193
Roasted Banana Rum Bundt Cake 63
Rum Raisin Bundt Cake 67
Spiced Coconut Oil Cake with Bourbon Glaze 162
Vanilla Bundt Cake with Bourbon-Vanilla Caramel Sauce 54
Vanilla Savarin 65
White Russian Bundt Cake 57

VANILLA

Basque Bundt Cake 129
Birthday Cake Bundt 147
Black-and-White Chocolate Marble Pound Cake 43
Black Cocoa Bundt Cake 47
Churro Bundt Cake 180
Classic Pound Cake 138
Classic Vanilla Pound Cake 126
Satsuma-Vanilla Bundt Cake 102
Tres Leches Pound Cake 140
Ultimate Cream Cheese-Vanilla Bean Pound Cake 142
Vanilla Bundt Cake with Bourbon-Vanilla Caramel Sauce 54
Vanilla Savarin 65

credits

Editorial
Editor-in-Chief Brian Hart Hoffman
VP/Culinary & Custom Content
Brooke Michael Bell
Group Creative Director Deanna Rippy Gardner
Managing Editor Sophia Jones
Associate Editor Kyle Grace Mills
Copy Editor Meg Lundberg
Editorial Assistant Alex Kolar

Test Kitchen Director
Irene Yeh

Food Stylists/Recipe Developers
Laura Crandall, J.R. Jacobson, Kathleen Kanen,
Tricia Manzanero, Vanessa Rocchio,
Taylor Franklin Wann

Assistant Food Stylist/Recipe Developer
Anita Simpson Spain

Senior Stylist
Sidney Bragiel

Stylists
Caroline Blum, Courtni Bodiford,
Lucy Finney, Mary Beth Jones,
Dorothy Walton

Photographers
Jim Bathie, William Dickey,
Stephanie Welbourne Steele

Contributing Photographers
Matt Armendariz, Stephen DeVries,
Eliesa Johnson, Alison Miksch, Joann Pai

Contributing Food Stylists/Recipe Developers
Marian Cooper Cairns, Mandy Dixon,
Jesse Tyler Ferguson, Rebecca Firth,
Kendall Smith Franchini, Kellie Gerber Kelley,
Erin Merhar, Ben Mims, Julie Tanous,
Marjorie Taylor

Cover
Photography by William Dickey
Recipe Development by Tricia Manzanero
Food Styling by Kellie Gerber Kelley
Styling by Sidney Bragiel